The Birds Talk to God

by

June Lauzon

Sketches by Connie French

Copyright   1992

by June K. Lauzon

Crowell House, Publisher
North Chatham, Mass.

Dedicated to My Children,
Grandchildren,
and
Great Grandchildren
who love nature as I do

"Do you ne're think what wondrous beings these?
do you ne're think who made them and who taught
the dialect they speak, where melodies alone
are the interpreters of thought?
Where household words are songs in many keys,
sweeter than instruments of man e're caught!
Whose habitations in the treetops
are halfway houses on the road to heaven?

Henry Wadsworth Longfellow
BIRDS OF KILLINGWORTH

"A bird's nest, mark it well, within, without,
No tool had that wrought, no knife to cut,
No nail to fix, no bodkin to insert,
No glue to fix, his little bill was all.
And yet how neatly finished! What nice hand,
With every implement and means of art,
And twenty years of apprenticeship to boot,
Could make me such another?"

         James Hurdis

"The flowers appear on the earth; the time
 of the singing of birds is come, and the voice
  of the turtle is heard in our land."

         Song of Solomon 2: 12

INTRODUCTION

Wasn't it Yeats' theme of the great birds that they might be closer to God than we humans — that they represent "spirits" who may have access to God in ways we don't?

In this book I try to show how each bird family is as different in looks, habits, temperaments and idiosyncrasies as humans. As I see a flight of birds overhead, steering their course to some distant destination, their signals and their cries are completely unintelligible to me. I understand little of their laws, their language or their policy. However, the more I know of nature the more I realize man's weakness and ignorance.

We can learn from the strength of the eagle to soar — to attain our dreams.

The little sparrow can teach us to trust

And the dove expresses peace.

It would be a dreary world without the birds.

CONTENTS

Preface 1	Starling 61
Bald Eagle 3	Rose Breasted
Sparrow 5	Grosbeak 63
Cardinal 7	Killdeer 65
Pigeon 9	Woodthrush . . .67
Nuthatch 11	Canada Goose . . .69
Robin 13	Osprey 71
Shrike 15	Chimney Swift . . .73
Hummingbird . . .17	Whippoorwill . . .75
Wren 19	Phoebe 77
Goldfinch 21	Catbird 79
Woodpecker 23	Purple Martin . . .81
Quail 25	Spotted Sandpiper .83
Crow 27	Towhee 85
Mockingbird 29	Mallard Duck . . .87
Mourning Dove . .31	Creeper 89
Screech Owl 33	Kingfisher 91
Barn Swallow . . .35	Ruffed Grouse . . .93
Tree Swallow . . .37	Seagull 95
Purple Grackle . .39	Pelican 97
Warbler 41	Penguin 99
Junco 43	Sanderling 101
Cowbird 45	Loon 103
Chickadee 47	Swan 105
Golden Plover . . .49	Snowy Egret . . . 107
Bluebird 51	Great Blue Heron 109
Blue Jay 53	Common Tern . . 111
Meadowlark 55	Woodstork . . . 113
Baltimore Oriole . .57	Epilogue 115
Roadrunner 59	

PREFACE
by
The Owl

Since the word "wise" has been attached to me, I have been elected to write the preface for this book.

I speak for all the birds when I say we are proud to be birds. Those who do not have wings cannot experience the exhilaration of flight under one's own power, or the glorious feeling of freedom as we soar over this beautiful land of ours.

We wonder if people realize what this world would be like without us? Insects, which are our food, would defoliate the trees and vegetation. The land would become barren. Crops of grain, vegetables and fruit might soon become impossible to grow. And would you not miss the flash of our colorful wings, and the music that fills the air with our songs?

Do people realize how threatened we feel when we see men carrying guns, bulldozing or spraying pesticides? Do they realize that humans are part of Nature's chain, and when they destroy a part of Nature they are destroying themselves?

Humans can learn a lot from birds. We are intelligent. We know how to do many things. What man could travel great distances in migration and find his way back to the very same place? How many humans show such devotion to their families as we do? Yet each bird family is as different in temperament, looks and habits as humans.

We feel a closeness to God, a feeling of intimacy and frankness. We can communicate with Him.

In this book we want to share with you some of our heartfelt talks with God.

Bald Eagle

Everyone knows
I am king of the birds,
elected in 1782 to be
the emblem of our country,
even though
Benjamin Franklin
favored the turkey!
I wonder why they call me bald,
when I have a head of
beautiful white feathers?
I am not popular
with the lesser birds.
Could it be that the more important one is
the more he is criticized?
Do you find it so with you, Lord?

Sparrow

I don't mean to complain, Lord,
but why was I made so mousey-looking?
I am pushed around a lot —
seconds at the feeders,
crumbs that have fallen.
Ground dining makes me nervous
because of the cats.
But I know you love me.
I never heard a song that said,
"His eye is on the Bluejay -
or the Cardinal".
Thank you, Lord,
for keeping your eye
on me.

Cardinal

"Whoit-whoit-whoit-wharty-wharty"
I am whistling your praises, Lord,
for making me so handsome,
particularly in the winter
when my bright red coat
stands out against the snow.
Wasn't there a Cardinal Somebody
who wore a red robe?
Was he named after me?
You will be glad to know, Lord,
that I watch over my children
as you watch over me.
I guide them when they leave the nest
while my mate builds a home
for our second brood.
Thank you, Lord,
for my many blessings.

Pigeon

My gratitude to you, Lord,
for making me
a city bird.
No soft, feathery nest for me;
a good, stout concrete ledge
is more to my liking.
I favor a nook or a niche —
wherever I can see
the passersby.
At the moment I'm living
in a busy Manhattan park,
cozy in a statue's beard.
Old men and children feed me.
The fountain's water
is sweet and clear.
Blessings on you, Lord,
for granting me the privilege
of being city-bred.

Nuthatch

People say
"There's that upside down bird
going headfirst down the tree.
It's a Nuthatch!"
One would think
the blood would rush to my head,
or that I would have dizzy spells,
but not at all.
I can do it because
you gave me large, strong feet.
I don't even use my tail
as a prop as Woodpeckers do.
How did you accomplish
such a miraculous thing, Lord?

Robin

Dear Lord, you must have loved the Robins,
you made so many of us.
We like people,
but we prefer earthworms.
Oh, the thrill of pulling a juicy fellow
out of the moist, green earth!
We are called Robin Redbreast,
although our breasts are more rust than red.
I thought about asking you
to change our name to Robin Rustbreast
but decided that euphony
was preferable to accuracy.

so, "Cheerily, cheerily, cheerily!"

Shrike

They call me the "butcher-bird".
It's not a very pleasant name, Lord.
Most of the birds avoid me.
I have no friends.
They must know
I have to eat.
Insects, birds and rodents
are my food.
But Lord, I live
as my parents taught me.
I do what my ancestors
have always done–
kill my prey by impaling.
I make a clean kill,
and eat what I catch.
Surely I have no reason to hide, do I, Lord?

Hummingbird

I am the tiniest of all the birds,
the elfin, or fairy, of the bird families.
I bathe in dew, shaking it
on my iridescent plumage.
My walnut-sized nests are fashioned
from milkweed down.
My eggs are the size of small pearls.
I am brilliance birdsonified!
I have achievements
no other bird can touch.
My wing-beats are 60 to 70 a second.
Also, what other bird can fly backwards
as well as forward, or even remain
motionless in the air?
I continue to wonder, dear Lord,
how you ever created such a miracle!

Wren

I cock my tail
over my back
and jump up and down,
up and down.
I'm nervous and worried
for life is not easy.
Look at my mate, Lord.
Why is she so fussy?
I toil to construct
a number of fine nests for her.
I escort her with pride
to inspect them.
She makes her choice,
then proceeds to rebuild —
so like a female!
I'm not really complaining,
for my cup runneth over.
I would have no other mate,
fussy though she is.

Goldfinch

I'm sometimes called a Thistle-bird,
a Yellow-bird, or a Wild Canary,
but I like Goldfinch best,
especially when my golden body
shines bright in the rays of the sun.
We have our babies
later than other birds
because we line our nests
with thistledown
which ripens in July or August.
Did I ever tell you, Lord,
that our nests are constructed
so perfectly
that they could even hold water?

Woodpecker

Why couldn't you have given me
a noiseless bill, Lord?
I hear people say
"Listen to that noisy bird.
I wish he'd stop that tapping."
Don't people know I have to eat
to keep alive?
I wish I could inform them
I am doing them a service
by eating their tree borers.
How could I make
my nest in the trees
without boring?
If you can think of another way,
I'm open to suggestion.
I have no musical voice,
but I can roll
a jubilant tremolo
in the mating season.

Quail

"Bob-White, Bob-Bob-White."
It's interesting, Lord,
how you chose us
to sing our names,
like "Whippoorwill" and "Phoebe".
We are proud that we
can people-talk.
But in hunting season
we find it best
to keep silent.
Thank you for our brown feathers
that look like leaves.
They protect us as we lie at night
in a circle in our leafy beds,
pointing our striped heads outward.
Thank you, Lord, for helping
to keep us safe,
and enabling us
to whistle our name,
"Bob-White, Bob-Bob-White."

Crow

Henry Ward Beecher said of us,
"If men wore feathers and wings
very few would be clever enough
to be crows."
He's right.
Yet some people call us rascals.
Mrs. Baxter shook her fist
when I nipped her silk stocking
off her clothesline
and pulled it through the air like a kite.
Farmer Jones put up a scarecrow
in his cornfield to keep me away.
Although we are not popular with some people,
others take us
into their homes for pets.
It's a puzzlement!
"Caw-caw-caw."

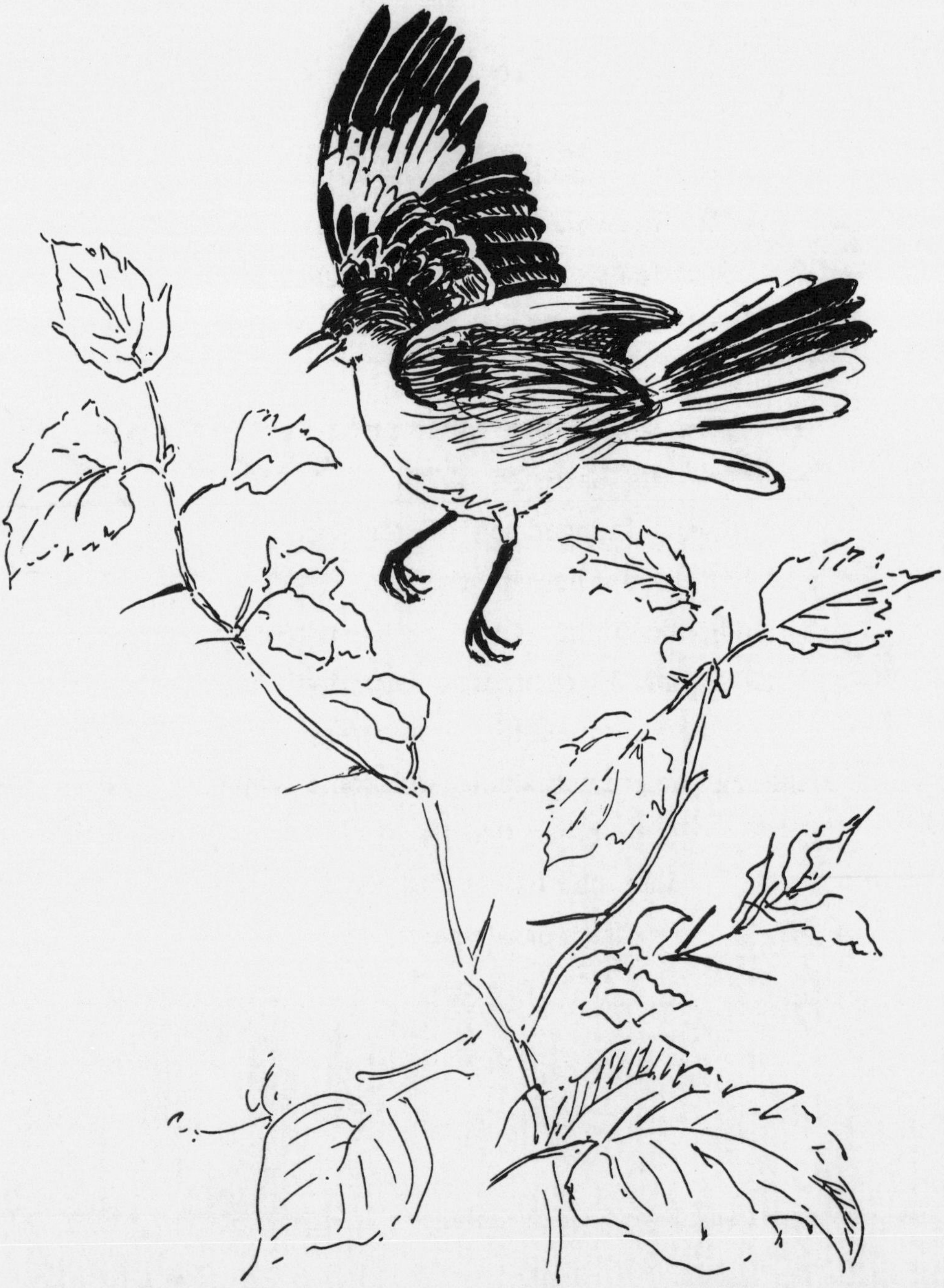

Mockingbird

I wish to make a confession, Lord,
You know how I like a good fight.
The other day I was so angry
at a bird that was mimicking me
that I flew madly at my own reflection,
knocking myself silly!
I wouldn't admit this to anyone
but you, Lord.
However, on the brighter side,
you gave me a great talent:
a master mimic!
I'm not an egotist,
I just know I'm good.
I can croak like a frog,
chirp like a cricket,
whistle like a person
and imitate my bird friends.
I can fool most of the people
most of the time,
but I can't fool you, Lord.

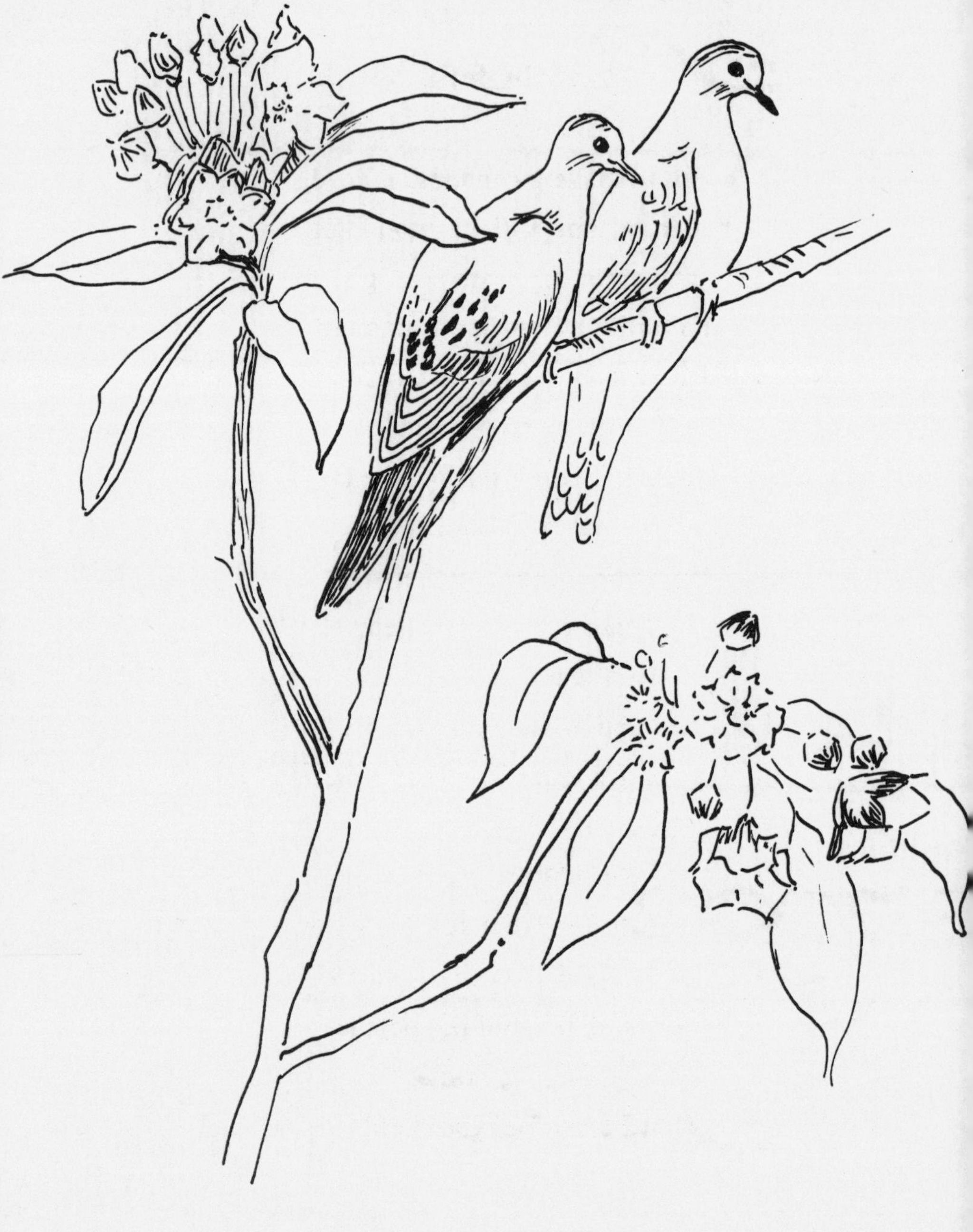

Mourning Dove

We are called mourning doves
because of our soft "woo-woo-woos."
Some say our call sounds melancholy
but we are happy, contented birds.
Sometimes I wish, Lord,
that you had given us a song
like the lark or the robin.
I tried to imitate the lark,
but had no luck at all.
I've also envied the mockingbird
he's so versatile.
Still, isn't cooing a sign of contentment?
We are important, however,
because we live on as a reminder
of the beautiful passenger pigeon
now extinct.
We have been protected by law.
We thank you, Lord,
for your protection.

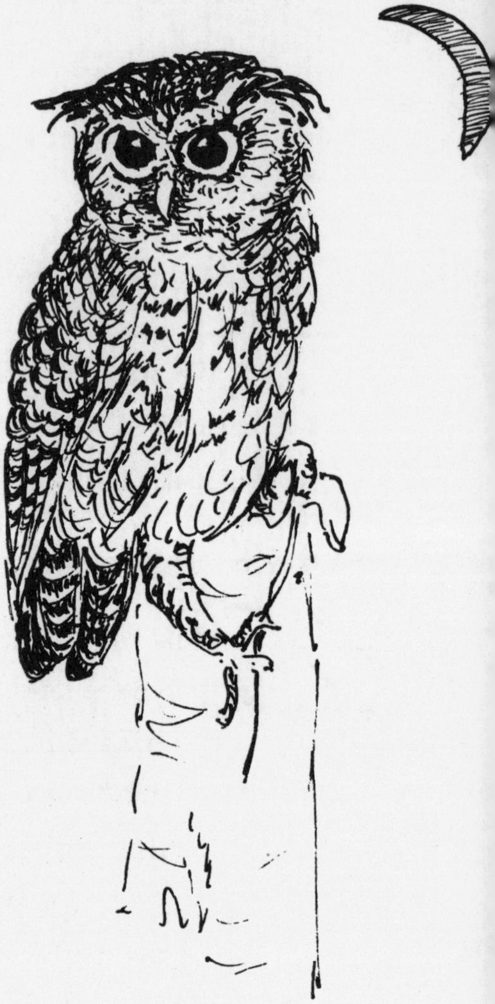

Screech Owl

I come from a large family,
I'm a screech owl
but I don't screech.
Mine's the lovely, tremulous wail,
"who-who-who",
half whistle, half voice,
that floats eerily on night air.
Why do people laugh when owls
rotate their heads?
We're lucky. We don't have to turn around
to see what's behind us.
We have other accomplishments —
we can catch mice,
snails and crayfish
in the dark.
I'm quite satisfied to be myself, dear Lord.
My grateful thanks to you.

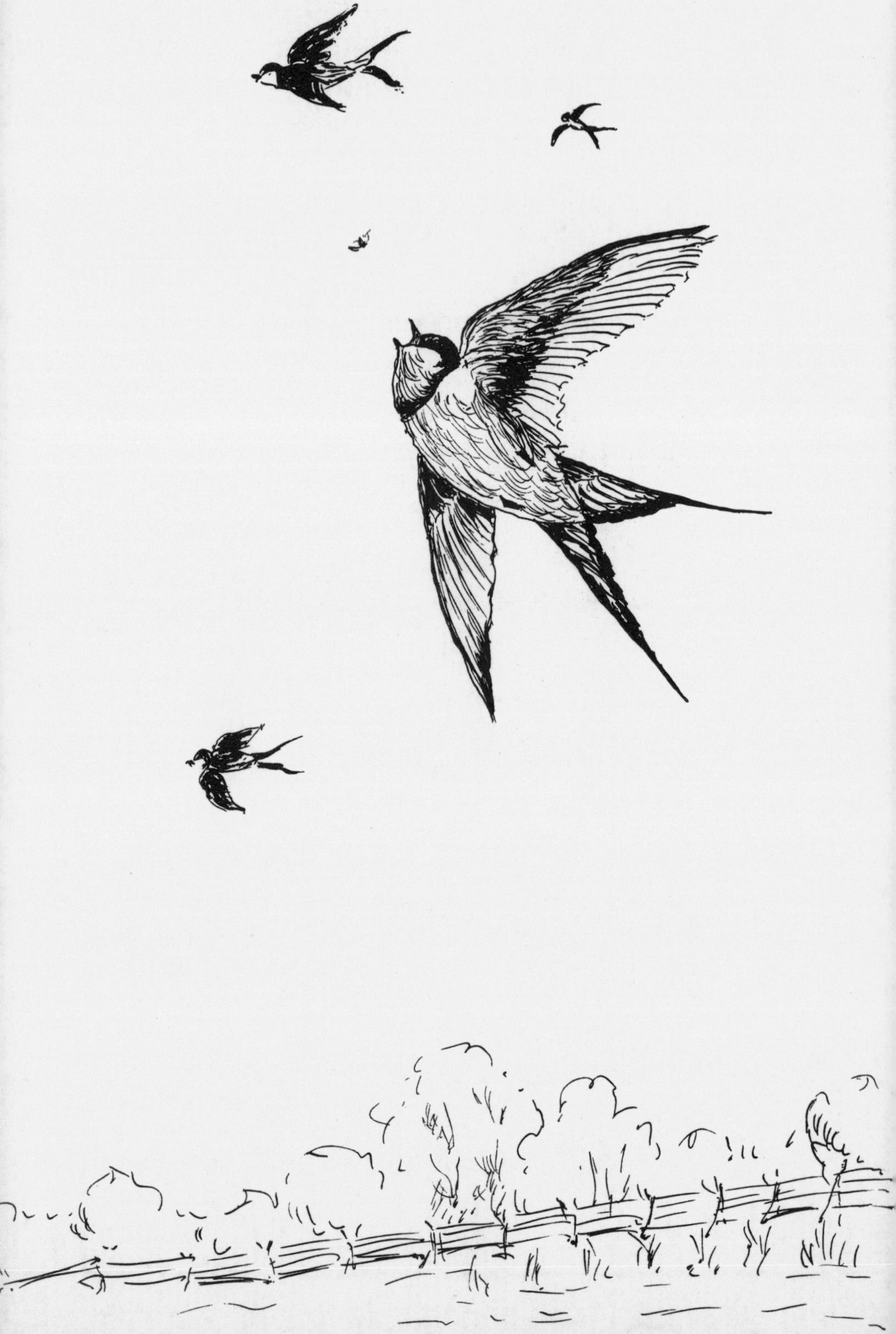

Barn Swallow

We are called Barns Swallows,
but just try to find barns anymore!
Now we have to settle for garages.
Should we not be renamed Garage Swallows?
We like our deeply-forked tails
and crescent wings.
We can catch bugs in our swift, zig-zag flight
of thirty miles an hour.
We like the life you have given us,
except for the lack of barns.
But think of the farmers
who have had to give up their farms
to make a better living!
We really shouldn't complain, Lord.

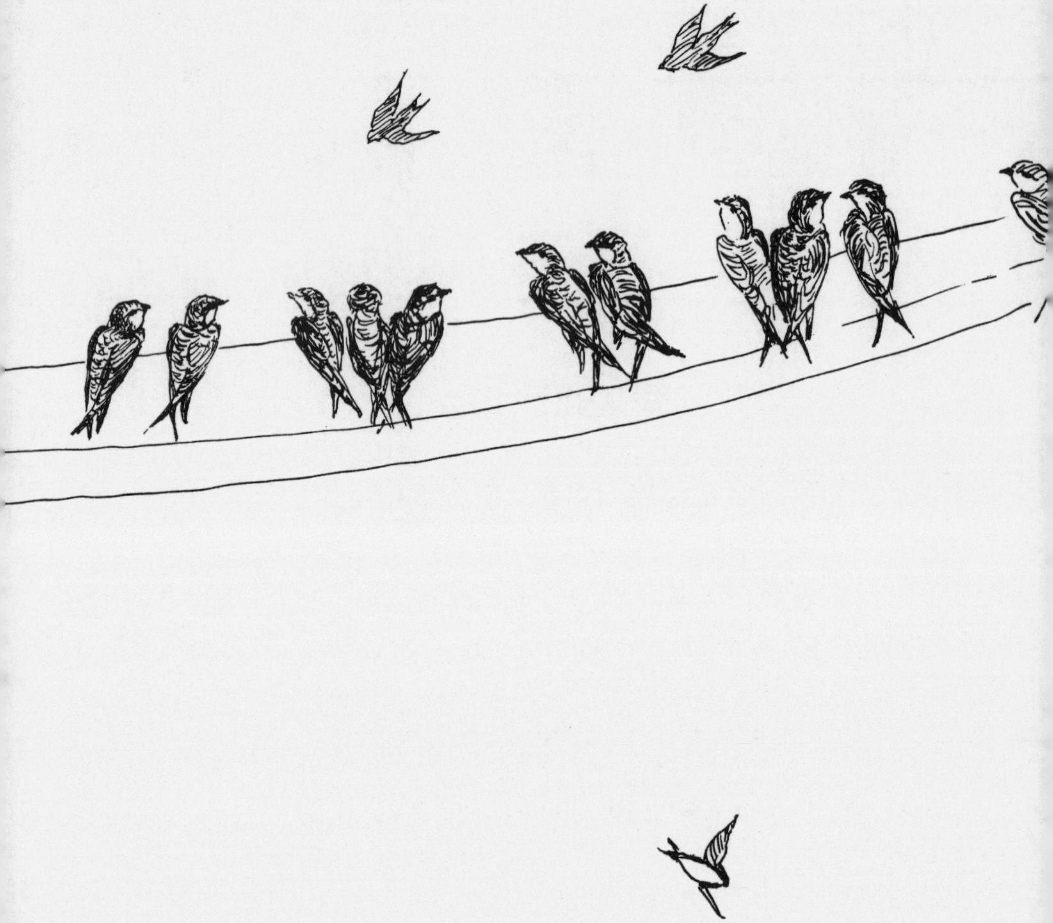

Tree Swallow

We are among the earliest birds
to arrive in the spring,
and the first to leave in the fall.
We are a lovely sight when the sun
plays on our greenish-blue bodies
and gleaming white breasts.
We travel in flocks.
Sometimes a thousand of us
line telephone wires
or glide in circles.
We nest in dead tree holes
or bird houses.
Our song may not be the most beautiful –
some say it sounds like a
shrill, high-pitched twittering,
but during the mating season
our notes make a wonderful, warbling sound.
We are a happy family,
and have no complaints, Lord.

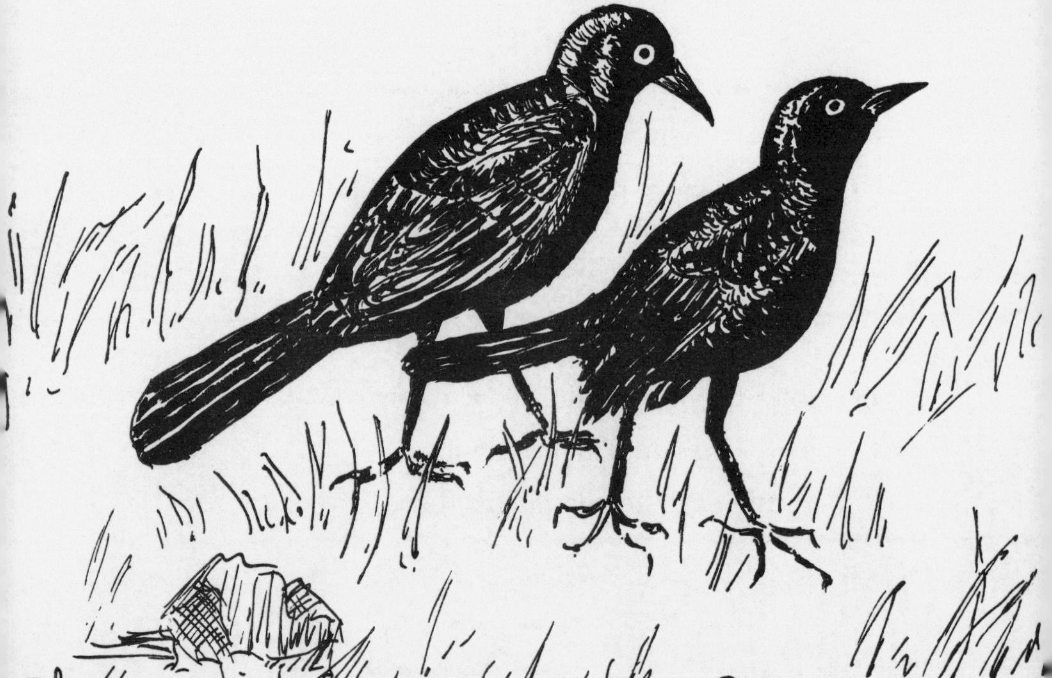

Purple Grackle

They say we creak and squawk,
sounding like a rusty garden gate!
They say we are arrogant
in the way we stalk about.
They say we
are naughty and mischievous
and do black deeds.
What do you think?
If you agree, Lord,
can you forgive us?

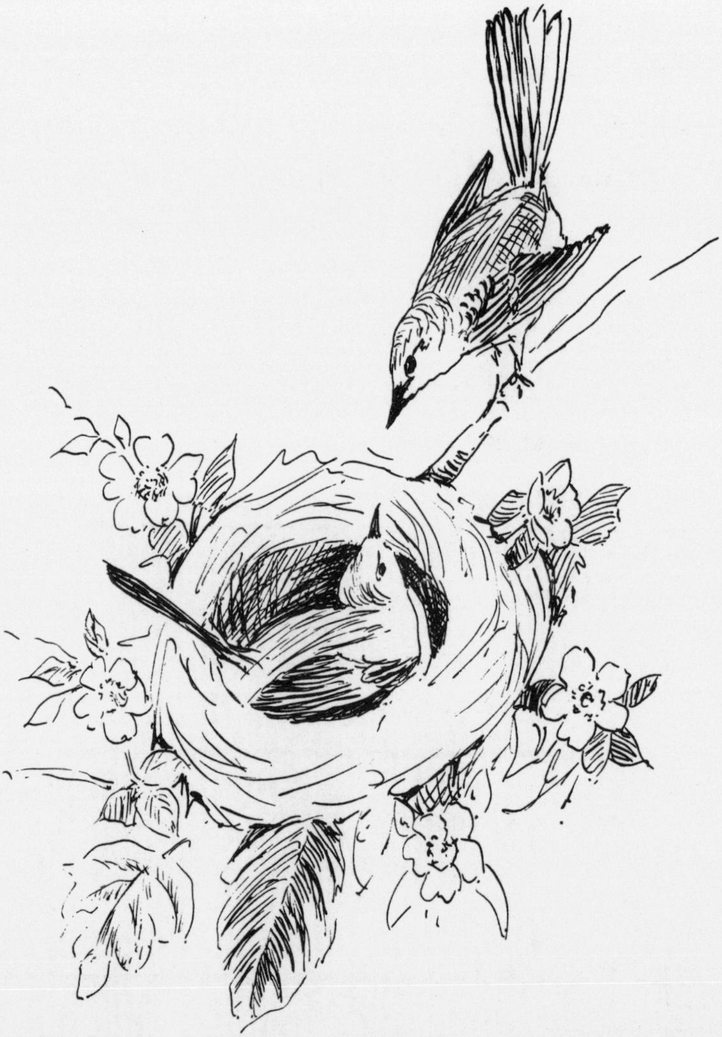

Warbler

There are many branches
in our warbler family,
but our song sounds different
in various countries.
Our Leaf Warbler cousin here seems to say
"chiff, chaff, chiff, chiff, chaff",
but in Finland the sound is
"til, tal, til, til, tal".
In Spain, it's
"sib, sab, sib, sib, sab",
and in Germany,
"zilp, zalp, zilp, zilp, zalp".
These things we cannot understand,
but we're sure you can, Lord.
Is it because humans
have different languages too?

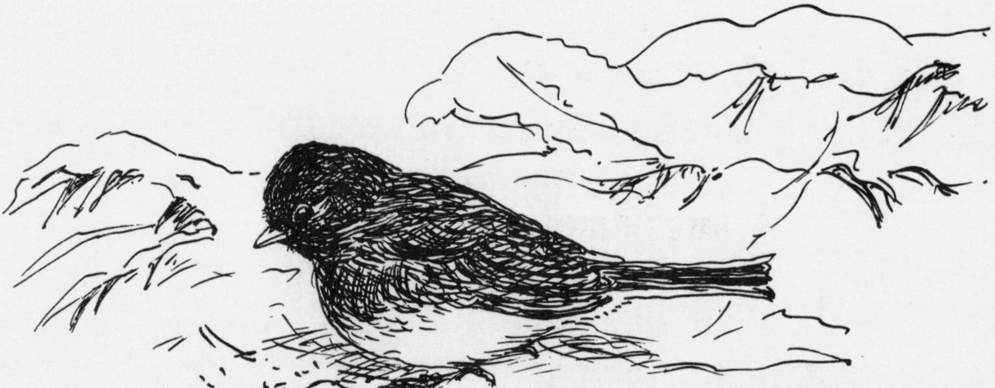

Junco

How I love the snow, Lord!
The beauty of it — the exhilaration —
to hop in its fluffiness —
to taste its deliciousness!
Why do people grumble about winter snow?
When leaden skies and cool, fall days
drive away many singing birds,
we stay to cheer people.
Then when apple trees
are tipped with pale, pink blossoms,
we leave for some cold, northern forest
and raise a family.
I am constantly in awe
of you, Lord,
for creating each bird family
so differently.

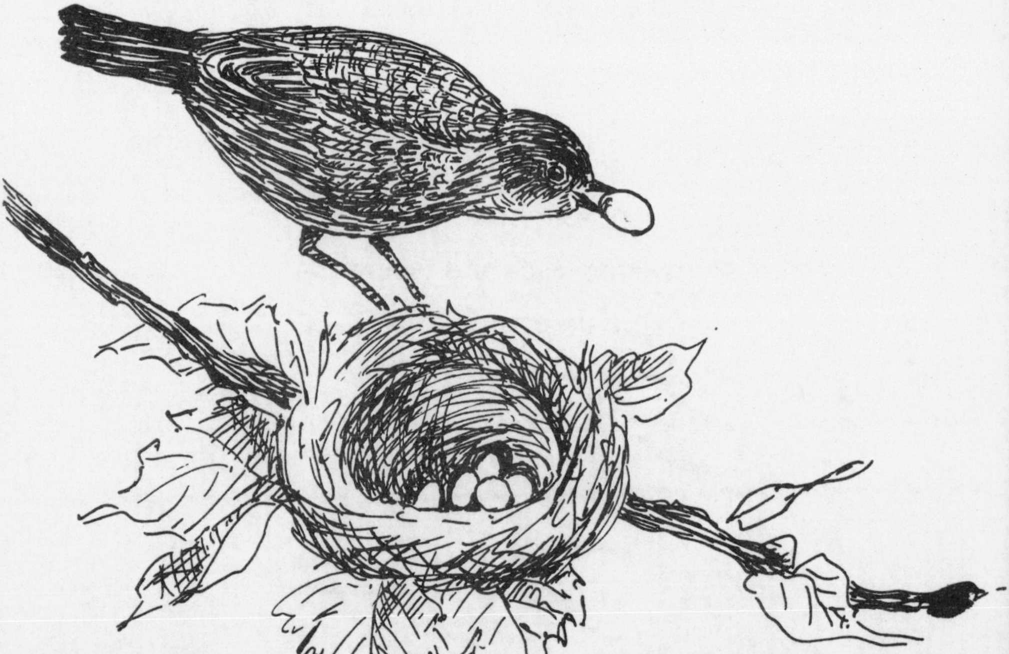

Cowbird

Is it wrong for us
to lay our eggs
in the nests
of other birds?
It's so much easier.
Our parents did this,
as did our grandparents.
Yet I sense antagonism.
A few birds like the Robin,
the Wren and the Catbird
recognize our eggs
and even toss them out!
It may be too late for us
to change this habit,
but I would still like
your advice, Lord.

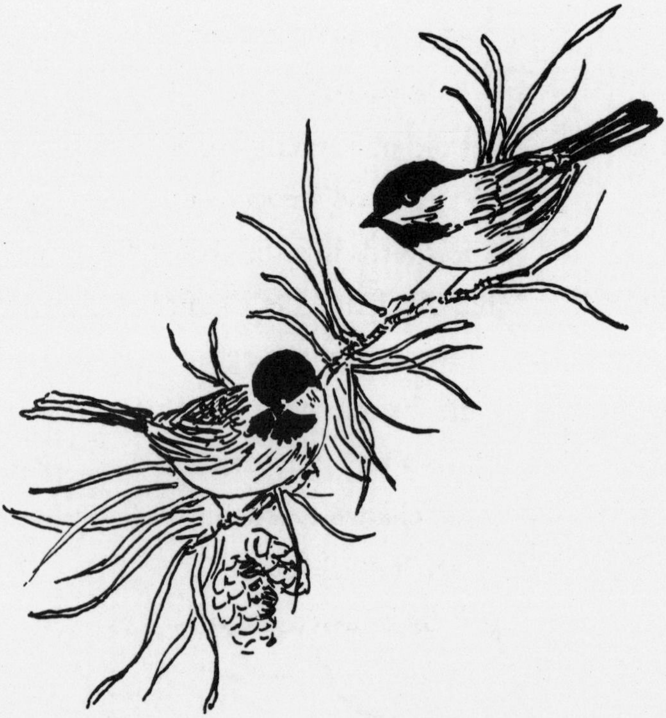

Chickadee

Life is too serious
to be taken seriously,
don't you think, Lord?
What's the good of going around
with a chip on your wing,
looking like an old sour bird?
We chickadees try to brighten
someone's life every day.
Why do humans rush around and worry so?
We are the winter cheerleaders,
the pepper-uppers, with our
"Chickadee-chickadee-chickadee-dee-dee."
By the way, Lord, could you
let people know
that we appreciate peanut butter
and sunflower seeds?

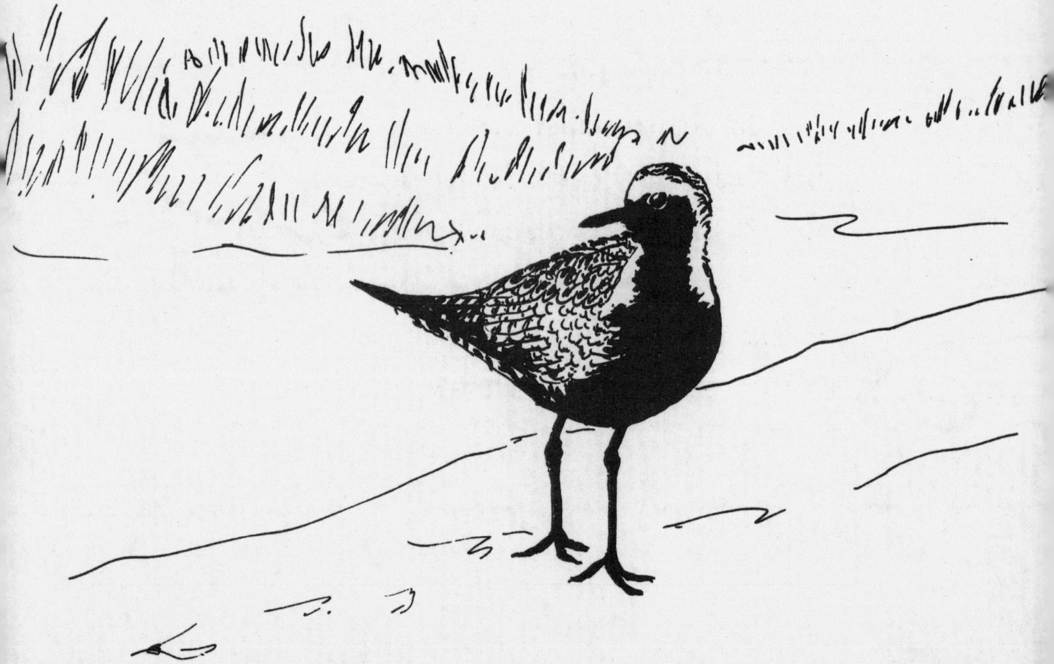

Golden Plover

Dear Lord, you gave us the distinction
of being the greatest travelers.
We fly far north
in great flocks to nest.
You did not intend us
to sit on tree limbs
because you gave us
only three toes,
all pointing forward.
We are waders.
Our feathers are beautiful –
black above, spotted with yellow.
In the autumn we change our color
to golden yellow,
like the leaves, the grain and the goldenrod.
Thank you, Lord, for all of these blessings.

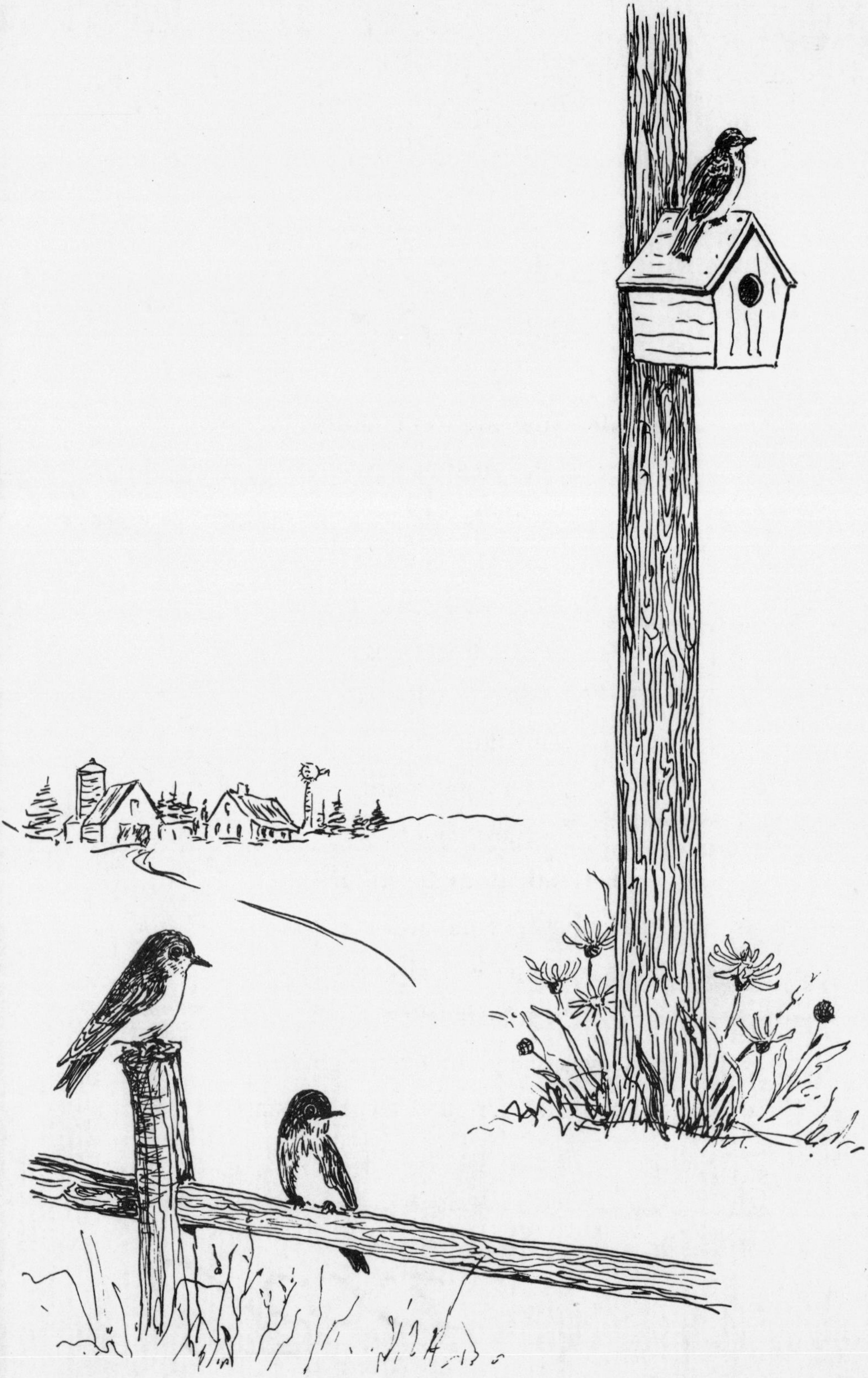

Bluebird

The early settlers called us
"the Blue Robins",
and Henry David Thoreau said that
we carry the sky on our backs.
Our vivid blue color rivals
the summer sky.
Our breasts reflect
the setting sun.
We try very hard to serve you
by spreading happiness,
because the world needs more joy.
But have you ever tried
to make that dour-faced raven,
that "nevermore" raven, smile?
We fail every time.
I guess it takes all kinds
to make a kingdom.
Bless you, Lord.
What a responsibility you must have!

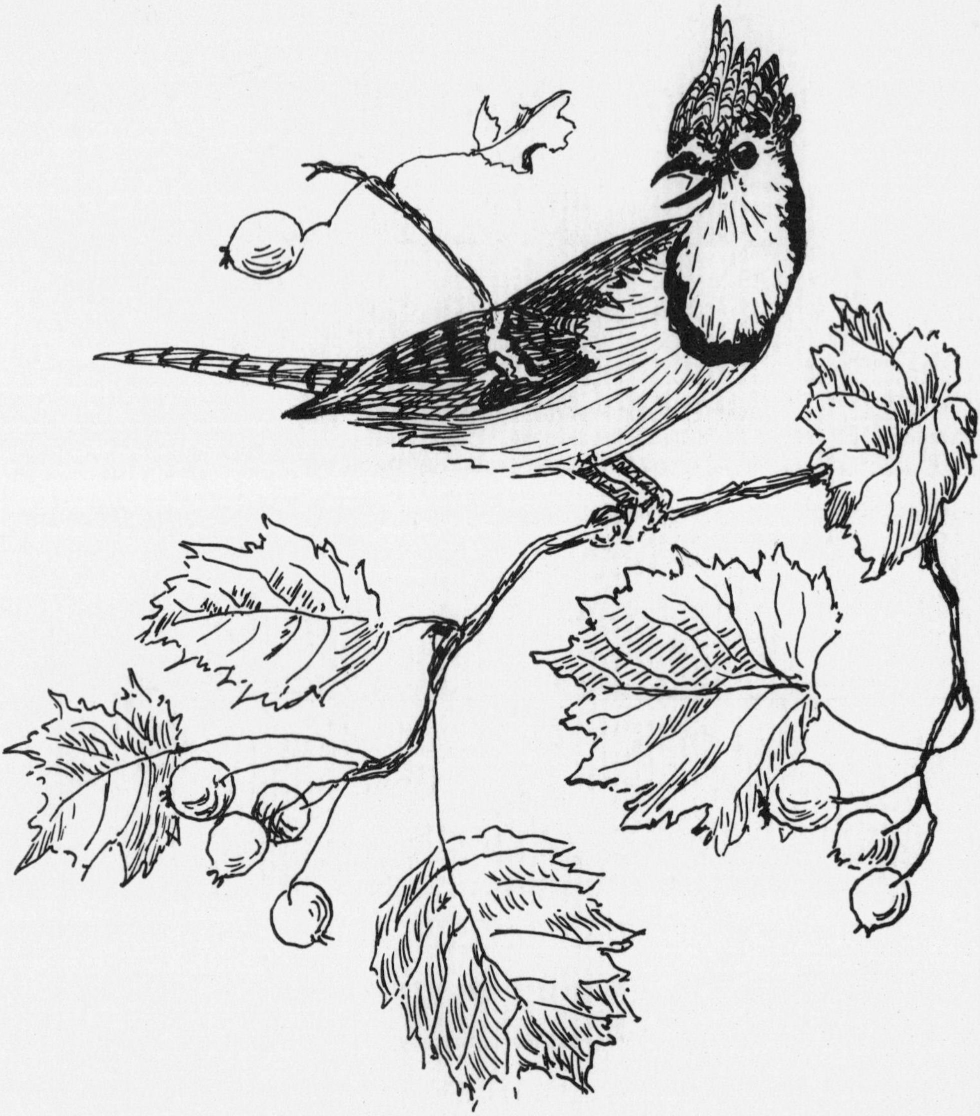

Blue Jay

Lord, I think I am a
dashing, fine fellow,
but many people call me
sassy and noisy.
They say I mind everybody's business!
But when I see someone
doing something wrong,
I like to give them a piece of my mind,
especially if it is an Owl or Hawk,
I like to call attention to it.
(I admit that I often
tease cats and scare snakes.)
Did you mean for me
to be a trouble-shooter?
It just seems to be my way.
However, very few birds
are more beautiful than I am.
For this, I thank you, Lord.

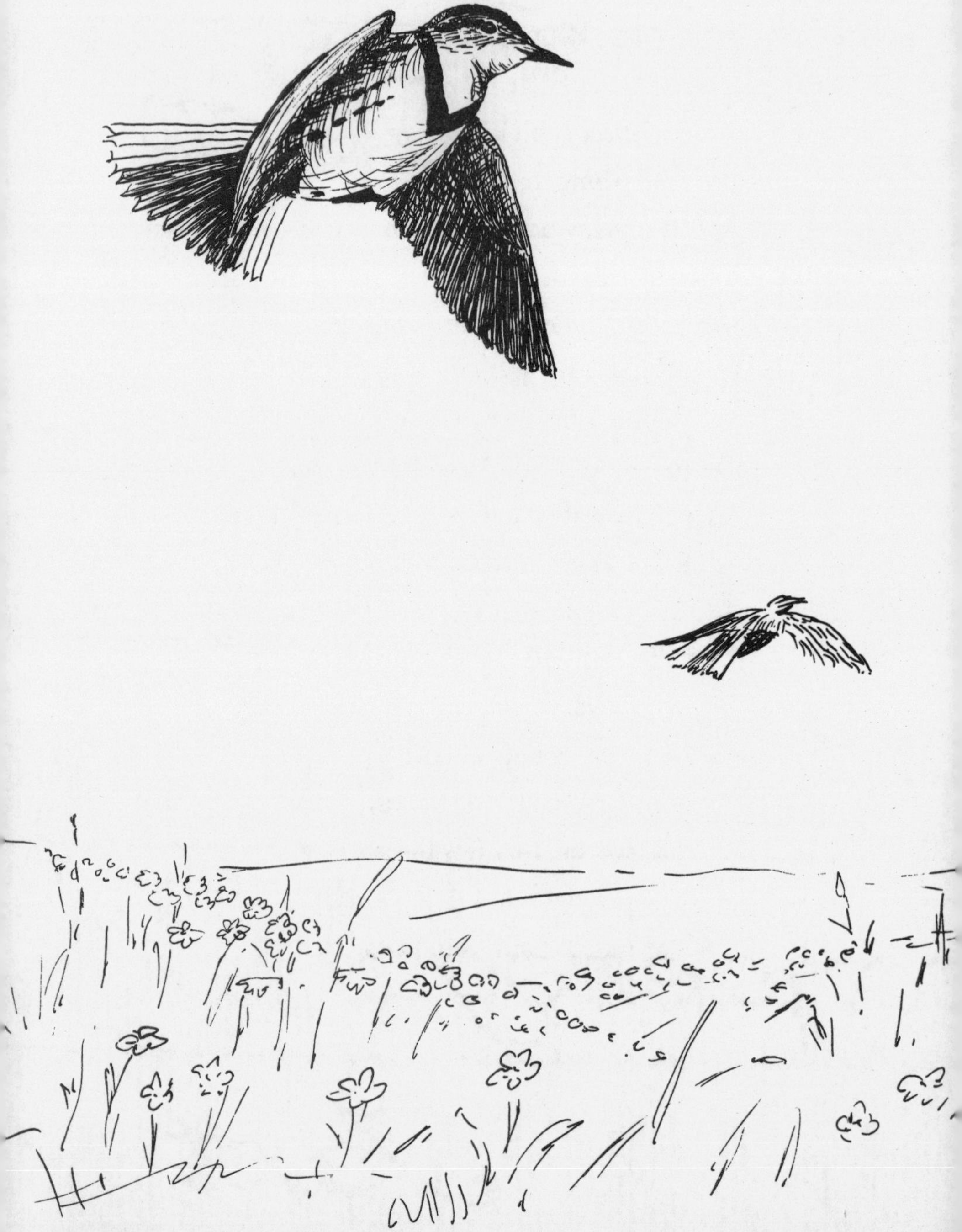

Meadowlark

Poets like Tennyson,
Shelley and Wadsworth
have been inspired by our songs.
Even my mate says she never could
build our nest
if I didn't serenade her.
People enjoy our flute-like,
cheery melodies.
They spot us
by the black "V"
on our bright, yellow breasts.
I do wonder, however,
about our lack of grace in the air.
We sail and flutter,
beating our wings
which are a bit stiff.
Is it possible, Lord,
that you intended us to be ground birds,
or do we just need more practice?

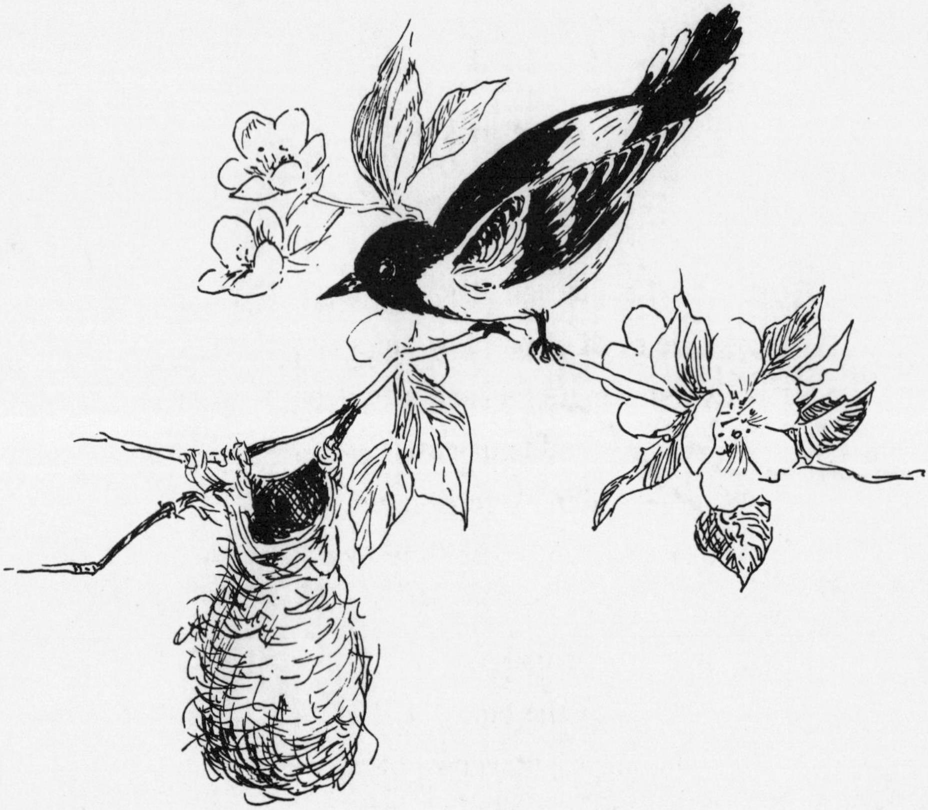

Baltimore Oriole

What striking colors you gave me, Lord –
black and orange,
like those of Lord Baltimore –
so aristocratic!
You made me a master builder, too.
I can't throw together
a few twigs and feathers
and call it a home.
A bird's nest is his castle.
If it is worth weaving at all,
it is worth weaving well.
I'm proud of the nests I build,
hanging long and narrow
from a forked branch.
Real conversation pieces,
don't you think, Lord?

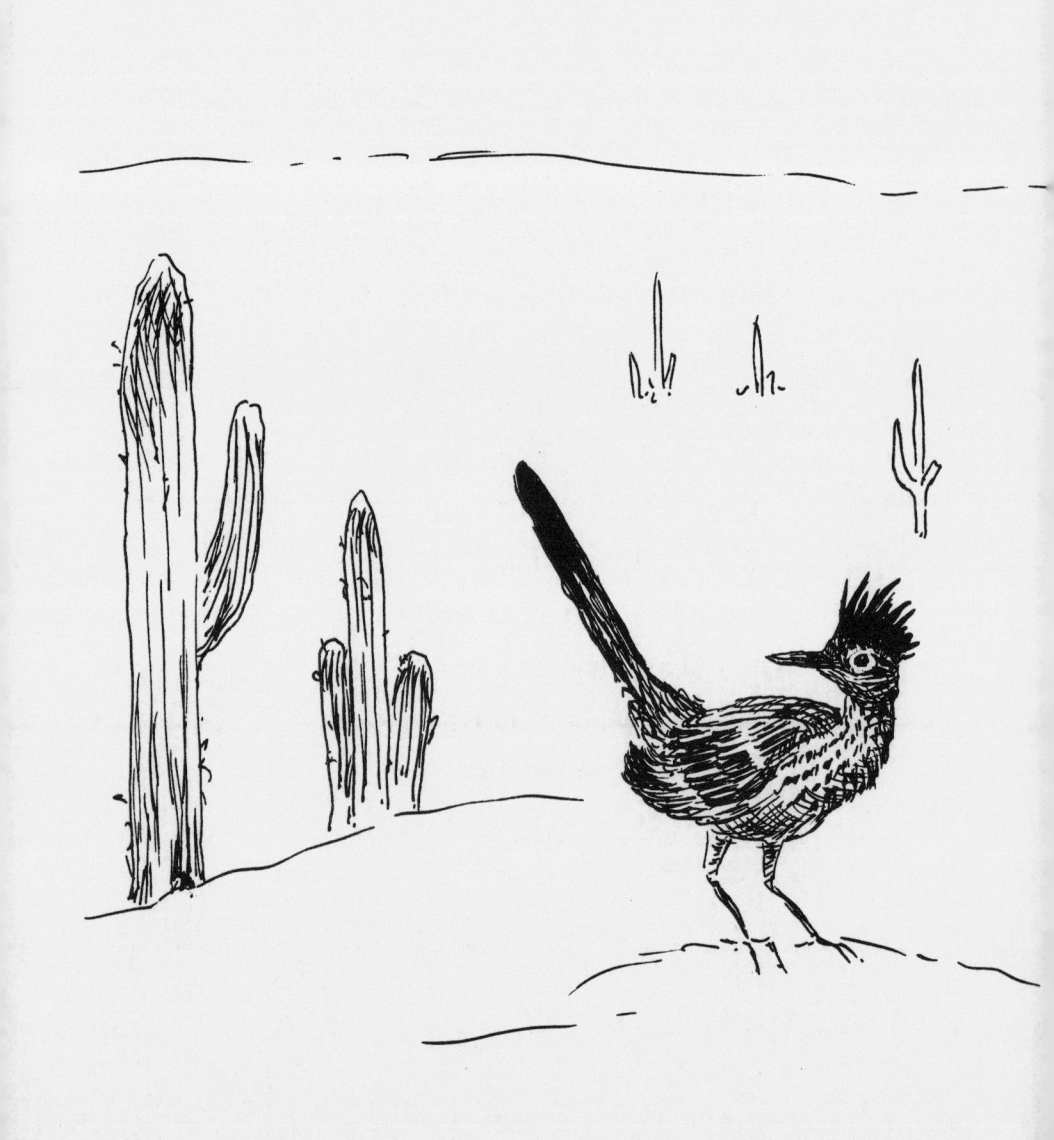

Roadrunner

Lord, I am not very much when it comes to
looks or flying,
but how I can run!
People say I'm an odd-looking creature
with a glint in my straw-colored eyes,
a crest that stands up as in fright,
and a long, long tail that acts
as a rudder and a brake.
Even though I am a bird,
I prefer to run.
Are you sure
you intended me to be a bird?
Actually, I don't mind.
I know you love me,

ugly as I am.

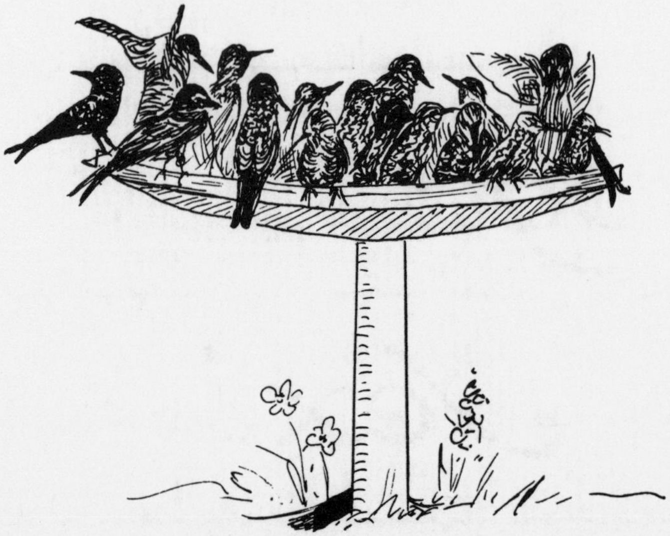

Starling

Lord, you created us
handsome in our metallic-like summer coats
and our spotted brown winter ones.
We were brought from Europe
in 1890
to free the trees from insects.
Since then we have procreated with enthusiasm.
Now man complains
that we have over-populated!
He says that we are noisy,
and build slovenly nests.
But we are good parents, Lord.
We care for our young,
Are our faults worse
than those of some people?

Rose-Breasted Grosbeak

Have you noticed, God,
that I am called a model husband?
I assist my mate in building her nest.
When she sits on the eggs,
I bring her food.
Sometimes I take over
the sitting myself.
People call me gentle and cheerful.
Farmers welcome me for eating
their harmful insects.
I like my rose bib
and black and white body.
Forgive my bragging, Lord,
But I wanted to be sure
you realized my good points.

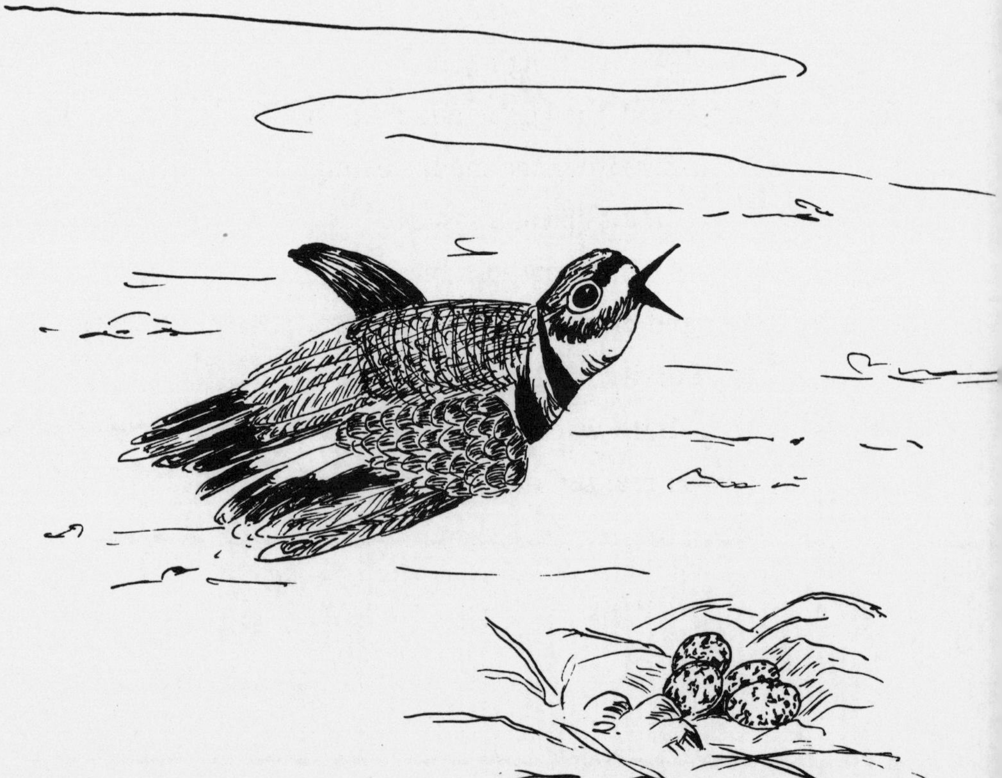

Killdeer

Remember me, Lord? I'm the bird
with the dark, double neck-rings
and tawny back
from the Plover family.
My call is a cheery "kill-<u>dee</u>-kill-<u>dee</u>".
Never could pronounce R!
My nest site is open ground.
Some might think it dangerous,
but you know my trick, Lord?
I lure intruders away
from my nesting site
by faking a broken wing.
A few hops while dragging my wing,
then a few more, and more,
until my intruder
is far enough away
from our hatching eggs.
A wonderful ruse,
wouldn't you say, Lord?

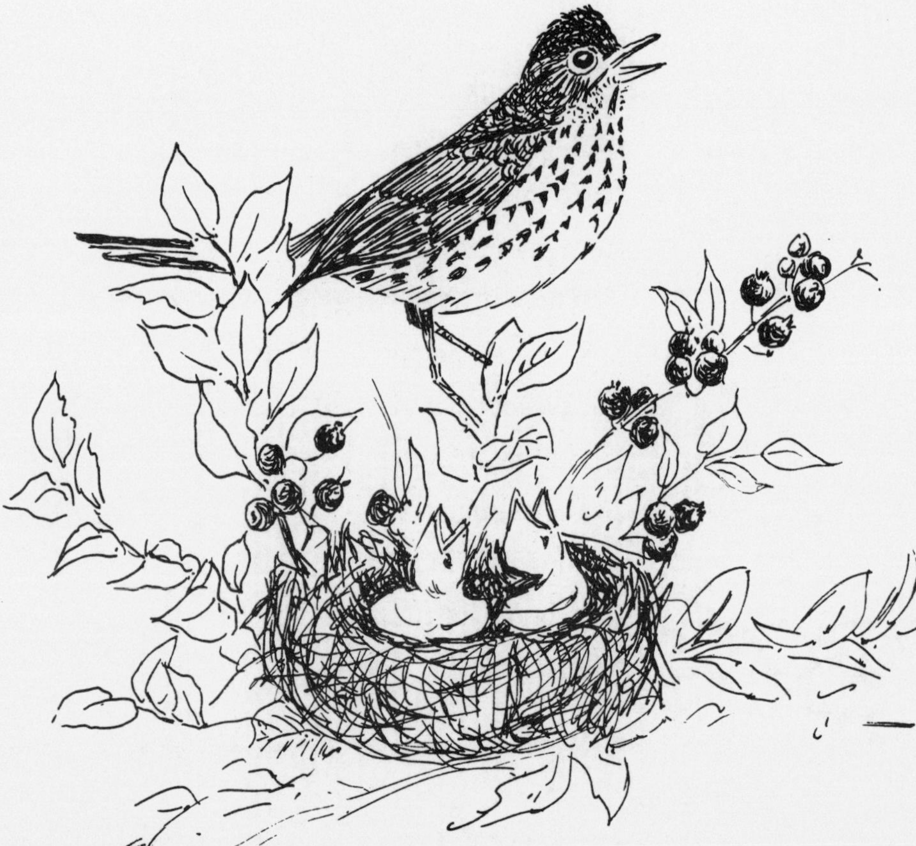

Wood Thrush

Dear Lord,
you gave us a beautiful voice.
At twilight our song
is flute-like and pleasing to people.
We never tire of singing.
One might say our song
is a theme with variations.
You also gave us
beautiful reddish-brown bodies
with spotted breasts.
For all of these things we thank you.
Each year I select
a different location for our nest.
This year our nest
is sunk in a bed of moss
under a blueberry bush.
This change adds interest to life,
don't you think Lord?

Canada Goose

Dear Lord, we are in flight now
from Hudson Bay towards the Gulf of Mexico.
About fifty of us are in wedge formation,
following our leader
who flies at the point of the "V".
Folks in the north say,
"Fall has come, there go the geese".
They can't mistake us.
We have long, black-stockinged necks,
white cheek patches
and sometimes a wingspread of five feet.
The blind, who cannot see us,
can hear our barking, honking chorus.
People wonder how we know
when to start our migration,
but one has to be a Canada Goose to know,
Right, Lord?

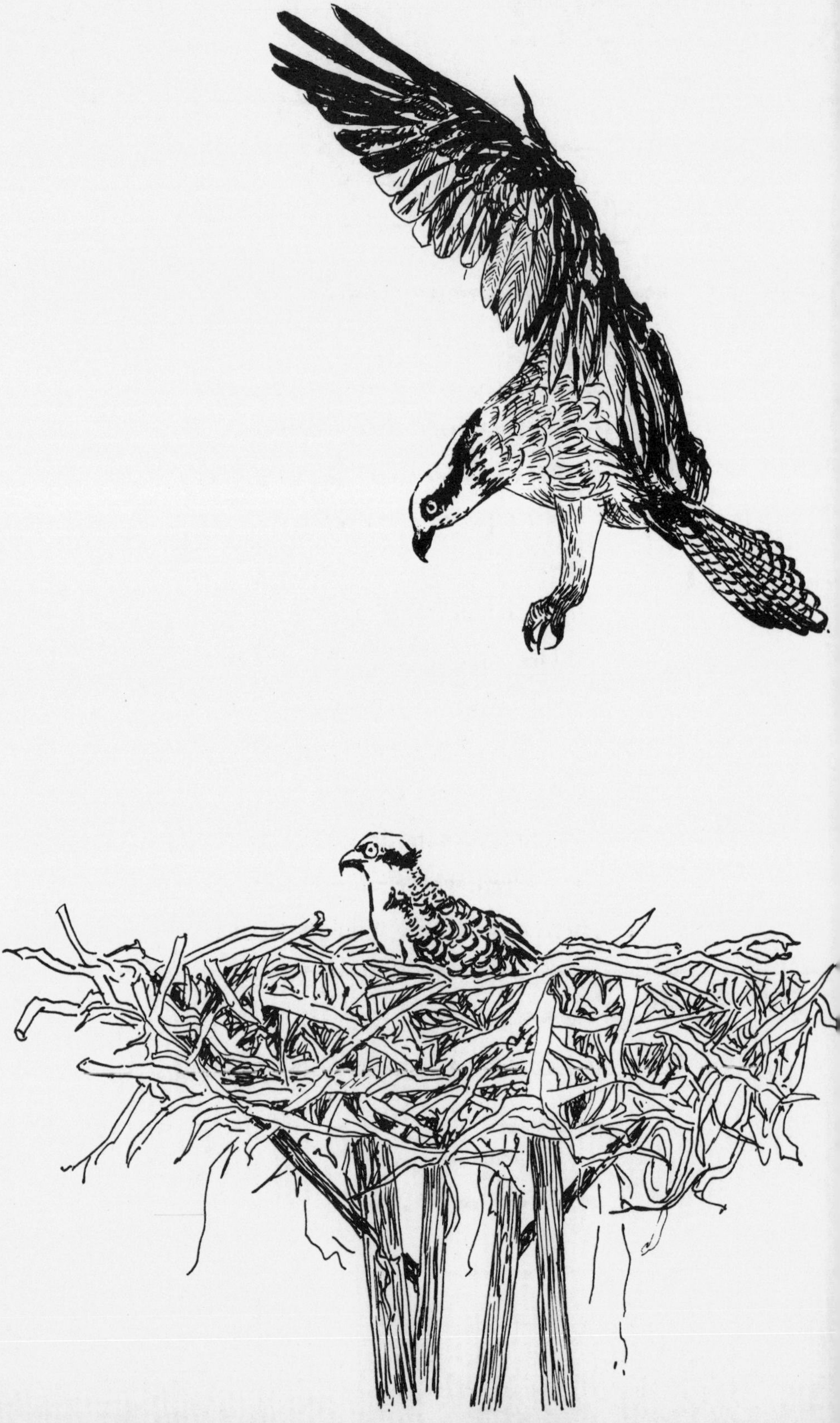

Osprey

Dear God,
I am not much for looks,
and my song is a high-pitched whistle,
but I am a solid bird-citizen,
minding my own affairs.
I don't molest the smaller birds.
I carry out my daily chores with skill,
especially chasing crows from the neighborhood.
Fish are my food,
caught by diving 30 to 100 feet
in salt or fresh water.
Farmers often erect tall poles,
inviting me to nest on top.
They seem to love me.
I hope that you do too.

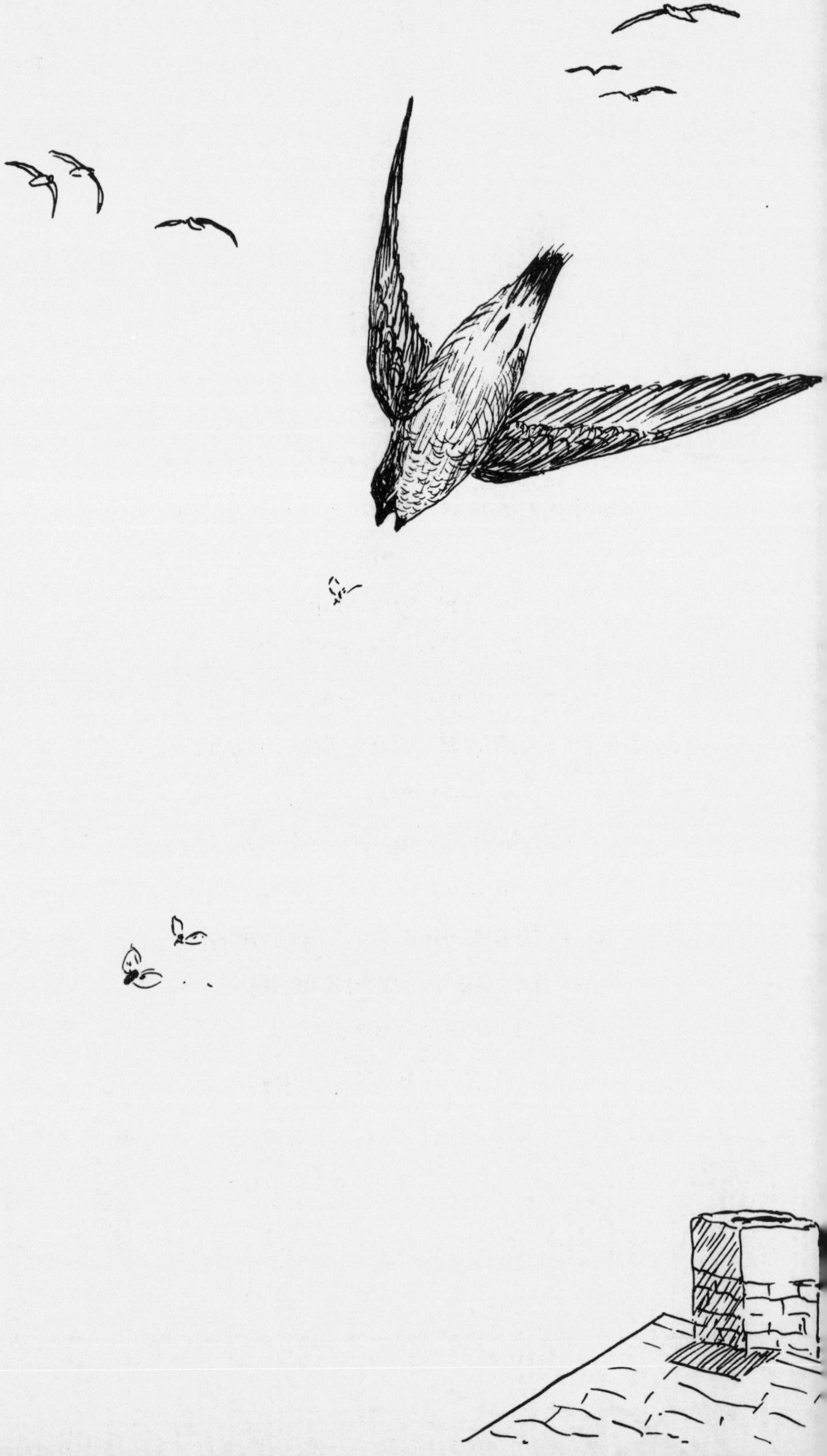

Chimney Swift

We are named well, Lord,
for we roost in chimneys.
We are not night birds,
but we prefer dusk, dawn,
and cloudy days.
We are sooty and stiff-winged
but are among the fastest birds.
We've been called
"the earth's speediest life-form."
We zig-zag through the air
catching flies, mosquitoes
and other insects
on the wing.
Sometimes we travel
a thousand miles on a summer's day!
We even do our courting in flight!
Do you think we should slow down, Lord?

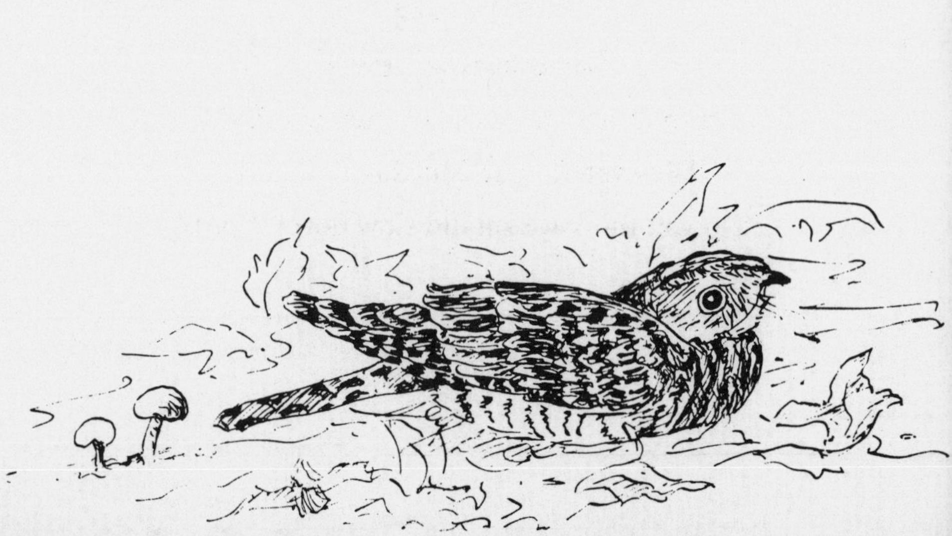

Whippoorwill

Did you know, God,
that I can call "Whippoorwill"
about 200 times
without stopping?
It may drive some people crazy,
but I am having fun.
Also, I'm so perfectly camouflaged
that I appear to be a fallen leaf,
matching the woodland floor.
We do not nest in trees.
We lay our eggs on wooded grounds.
During the day
we sleep in thickets.
Of course you know all this.
The diversity of
each bird family
is truly wonderful.

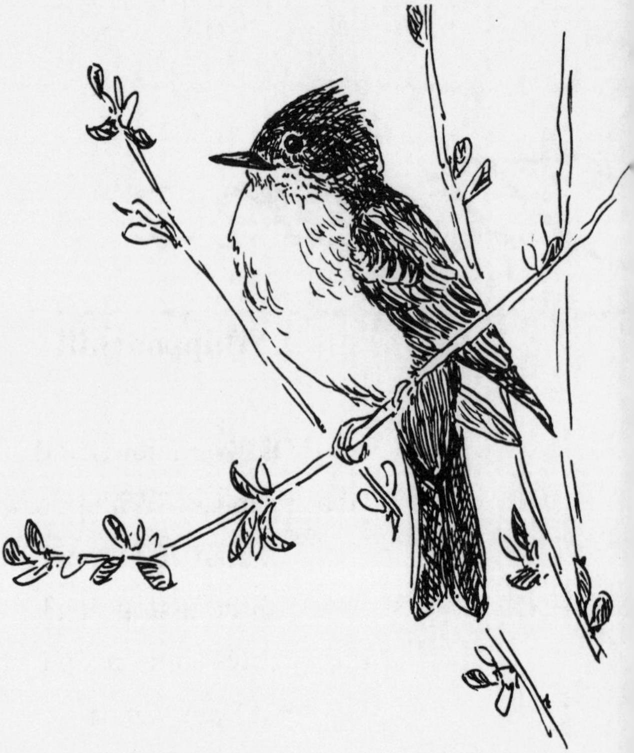

Phoebe

As you know, Lord,
I am one of the little birds
that come to watch
the Eastern spring arrive
during the first warm sunny days,
when swarms of gnats
spiral through the air.
I am a friend of the farmer,
eating his moths and flies,
ants, wasps, and beetles.
Year after year I return
to the same nesting site.
I enjoy the life
you have given me,
"Fee-<u>bee</u>...Fee-<u>bee</u>".
I bob my tail in praise of you.

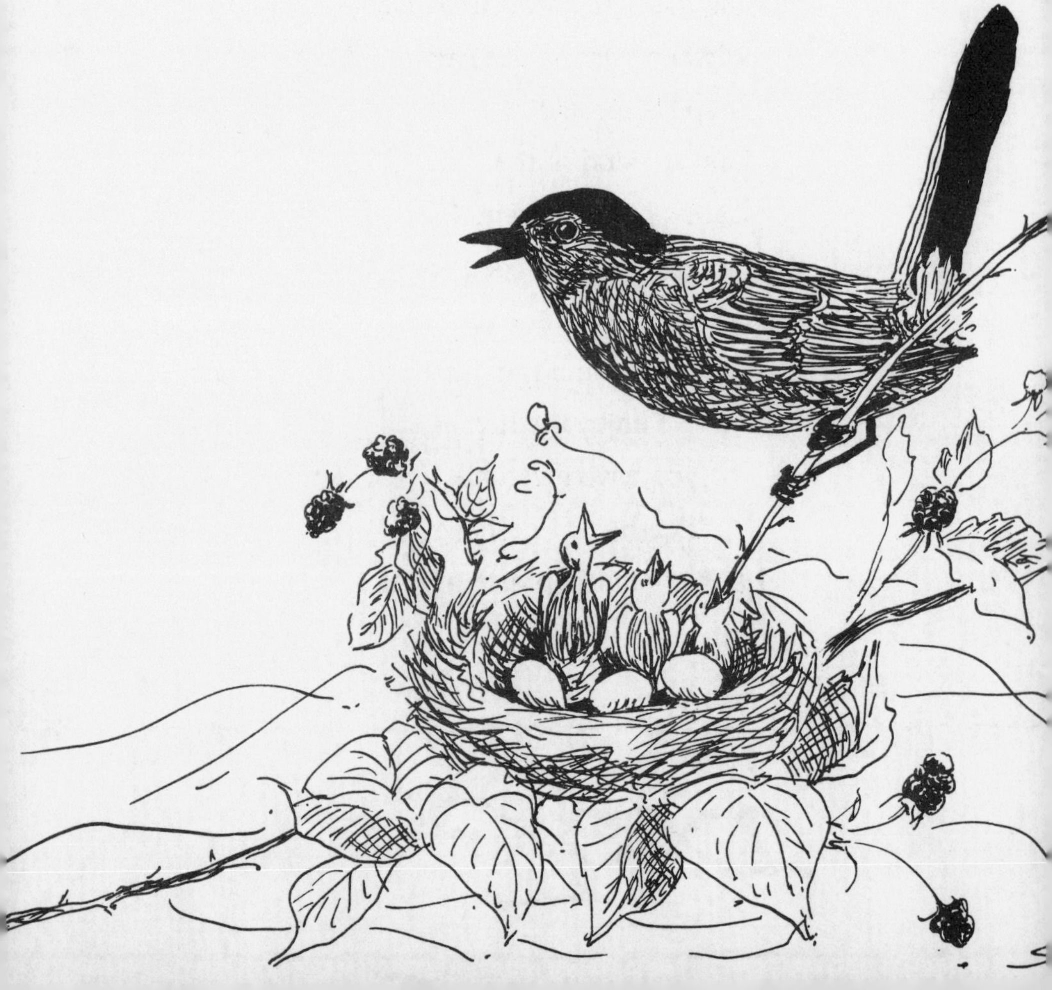

Catbird

Why was I named "Catbird?"
You know how I hate cats!
Was it because of
my catlike, mewing note?
However, I am thankful you gave me
a slate-gray, protective coat,
because I build my nest
among the low-growing,
tangled vines and briars.
People say I am pugnacious,
but I am defending my territory
by song, chases, body-fluff
and my raised wing.
Perhaps I should overlook my name
and thank you for
my protective advantages.
So, thank you, dear Lord.

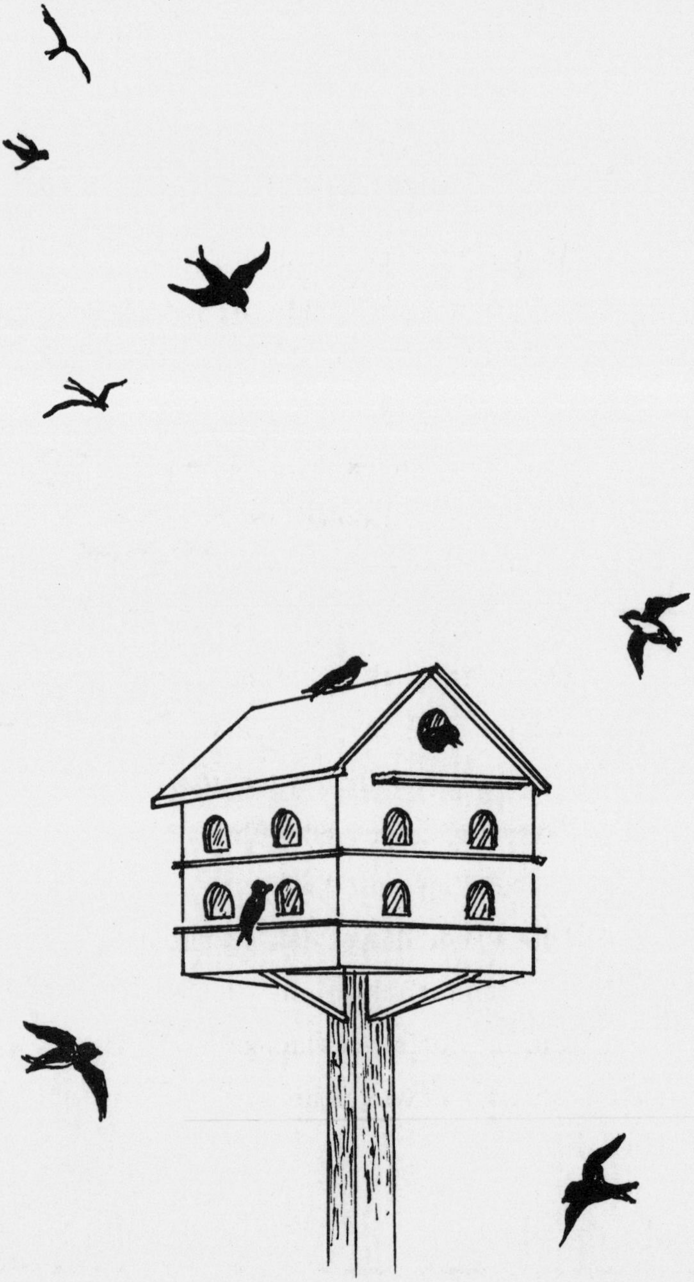

Purple Martin

As we gather in clusters,
purple iridescence
glistens from our heads and wing tips.
Some think we are gossipers,
but it is only delightful chatter.
Our song is a low-pitched
liquid, rolling twitter.
We enjoy colonizing,
but we do not believe
in exchanging mates.
We need more nesting places like
apartment bird houses
for several families.
Do you remember, Lord, how years ago
the Indians hung out gourds for us?
Please tell folks we could use some today.

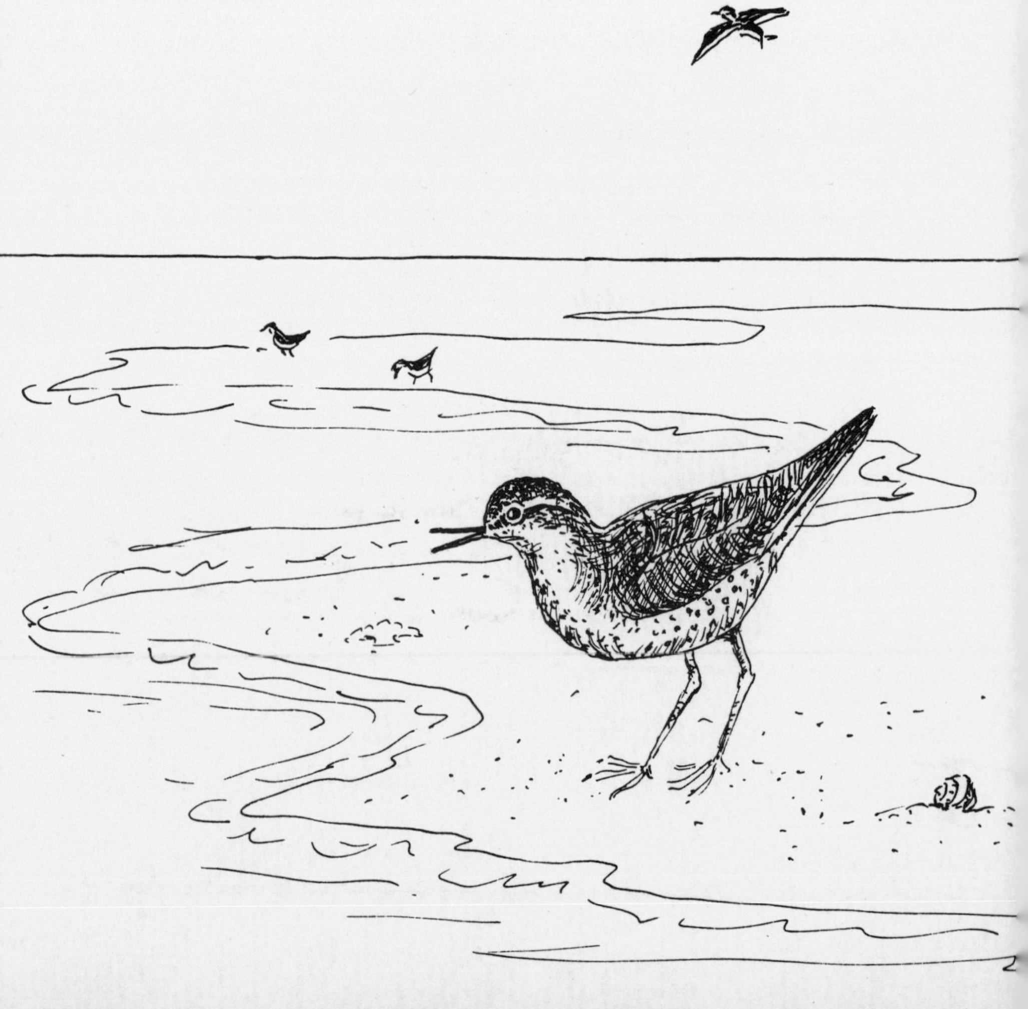

Spotted Sandpiper

I hope you remember me, Lord.
I am called "Teeter-Tail"
because I constantly lower my head
and raise my tail,
like a see-saw.
I run along the sea's frothy water-line,
searching for worms and spiders,
insects and small crustaceans.
The blackish spots on my white breast
vanish before the fall migration.
A slight depression lined with grass
is my usual nesting place.
"Sweet-sweet" is my call.
I just didn't want you to forget me, Lord…

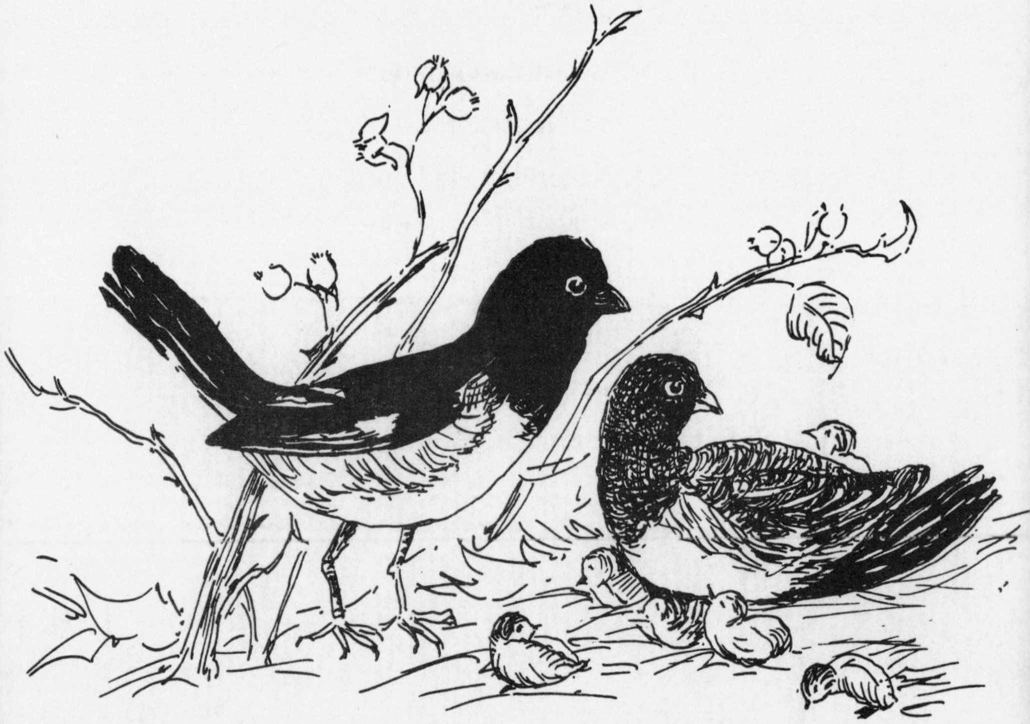

Towhee

I love the tangled undergrowth
of a cool, moist forest glade
where ferns and vines
and mossy greenery abound.
Your fallen trees provide
cavities for our nesting.
But sometimes I cannot find
these natural nesting places.
I go from place to place
before I find a cavity in a fallen tree.
Why are our forests disappearing, Lord?
Can you tell people we need them to live,
and they need us to live?

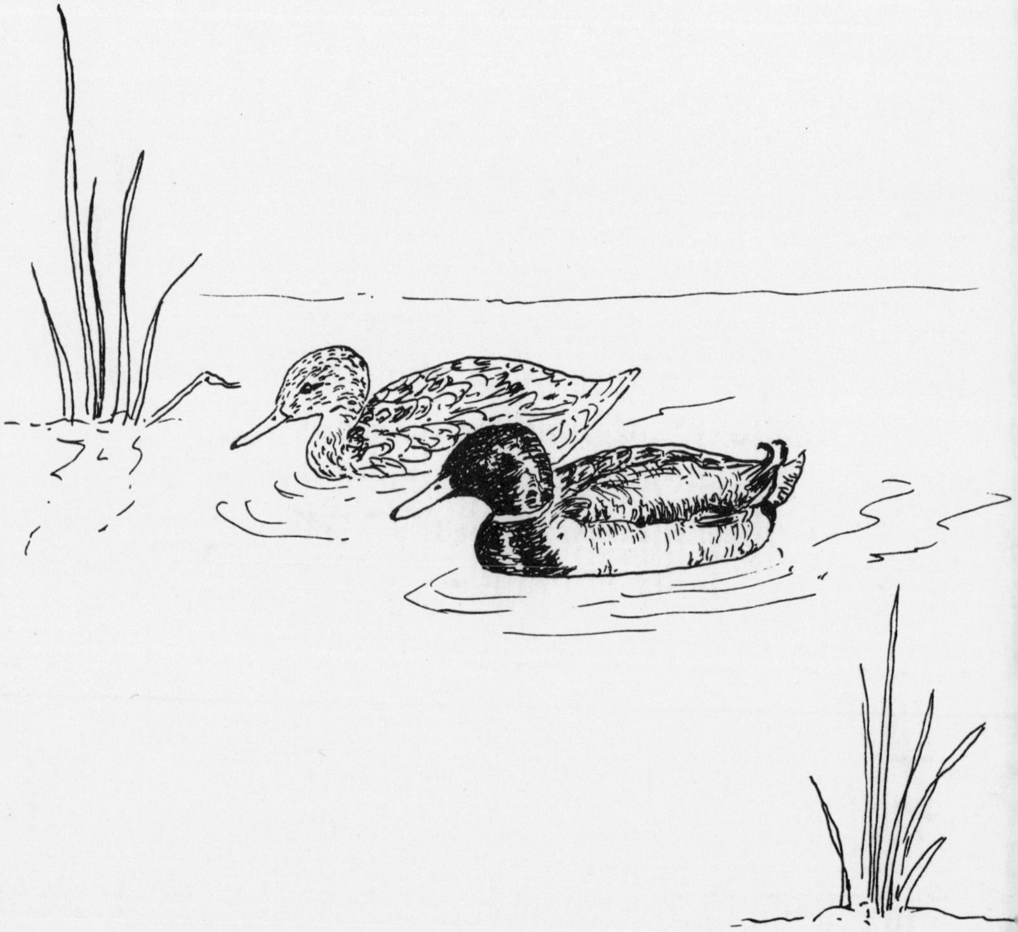

Mallard Duck

We are the most numerous
of the duck family—
one of the first to be
domesticated by Man.
Our population was decreasing until
the United States and Great Britain
gave us treaty rights.
Now we are protected
from people with guns,
except for brief periods in the year.
I am a lusty fellow
and raise a big family.
Mrs. Mallard lays at least nine or ten eggs—
sometimes as many as fourteen!
We have no need to complain,
so thank you, dear God.

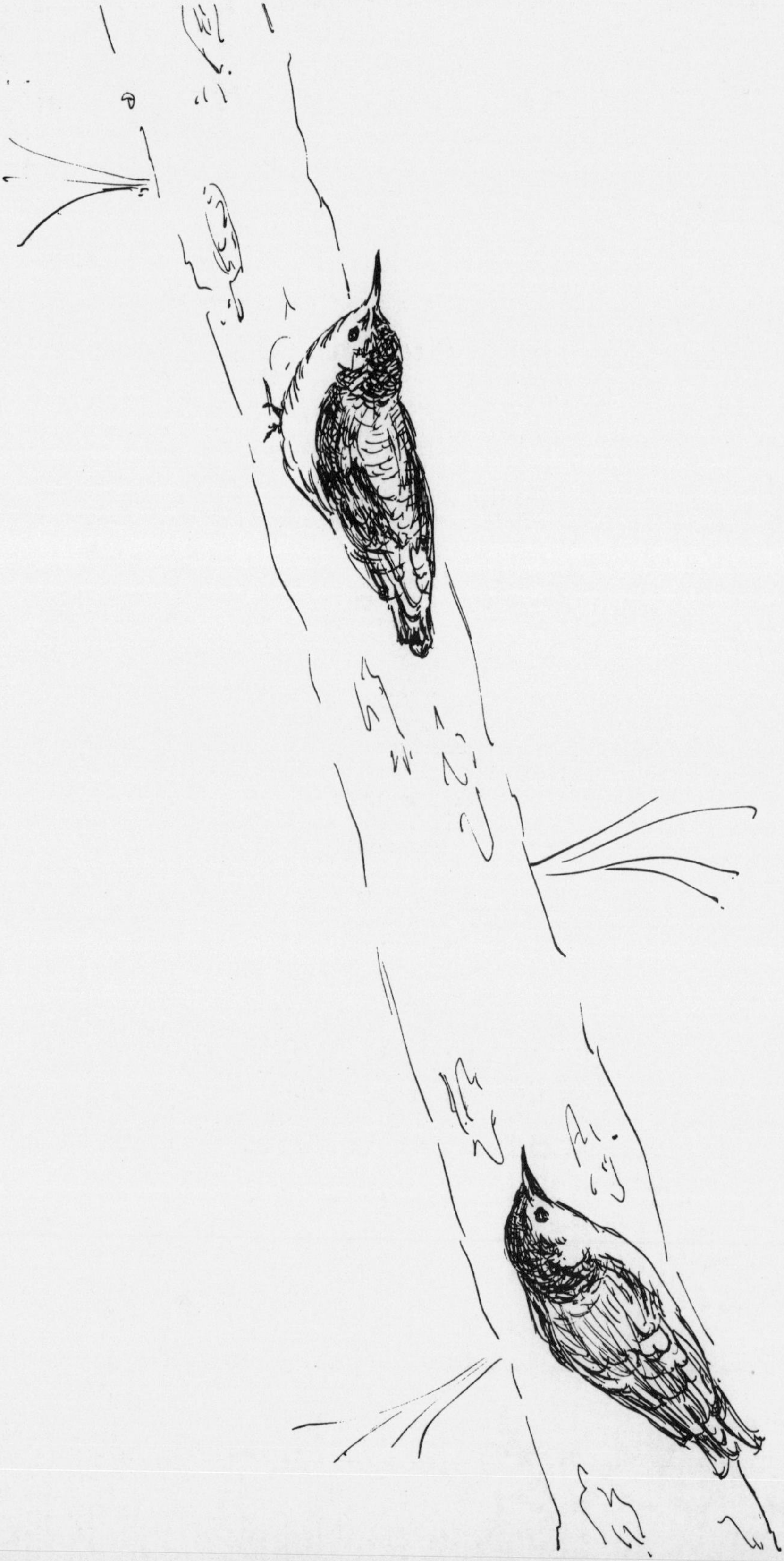

Creeper

Don't forget us, God —
we are your tiny birds,
light breasted, brown back flecked with white.
We use the stiff points
on our long tail feathers
as props to circle around and up
the trees,
as our long, curving bills
find insect eggs.
Our call is
"skreet-skreet, skreet-skreet".
Isn't there a saying that says
"Good things come in small packages?"

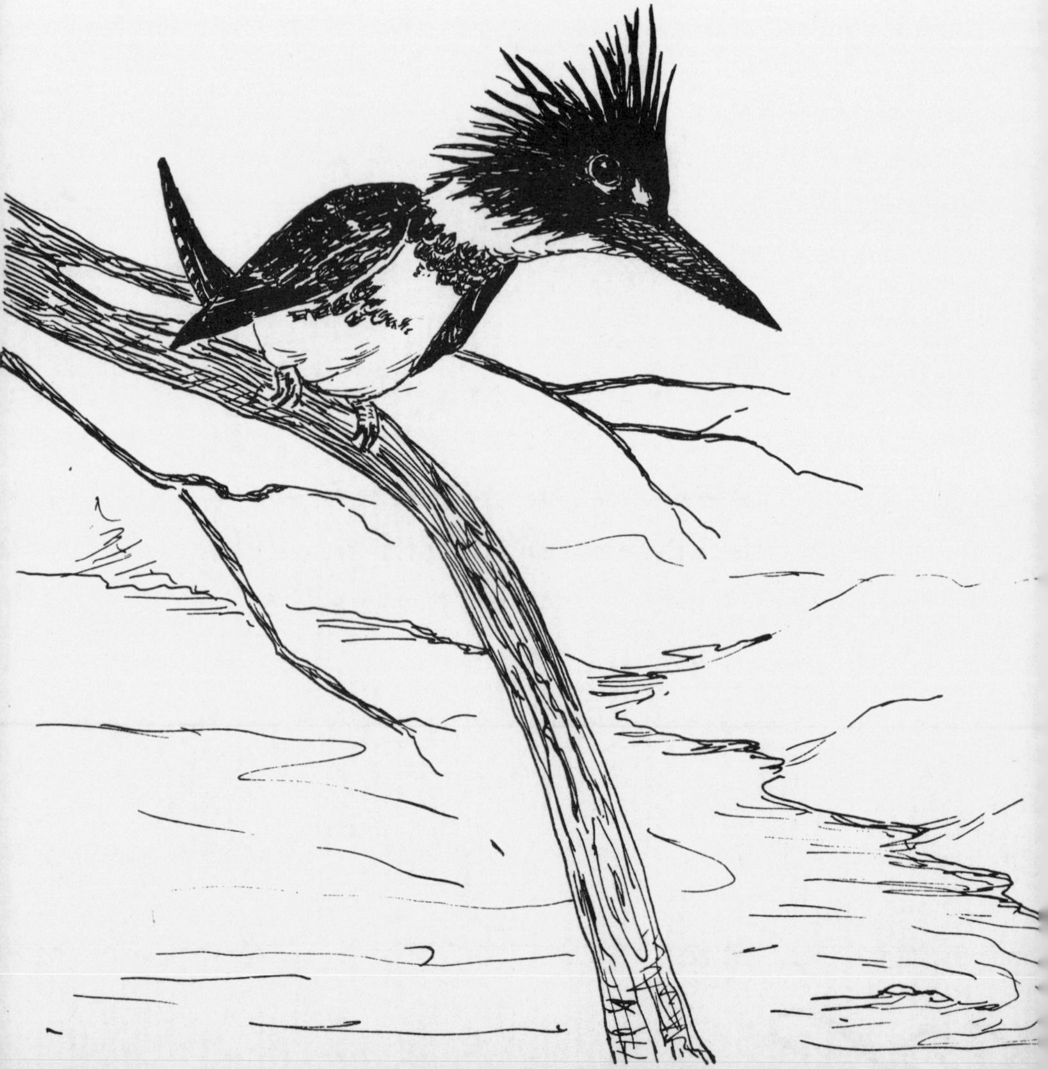

Kingfisher

We are fisher-birds
as our name implies.
Our caps are plumed
above our blue-gray bodies,
and our bills are sword-like.
We dig long tunnels
in sand banks,
laying our eggs at the terminus.
We keep watch along river banks,
ponds and shining lakes.
When we glimpse a fin,
we plunge in for the catch.
Thank you for our bills, Lord.
They're so useful in feeding our families.

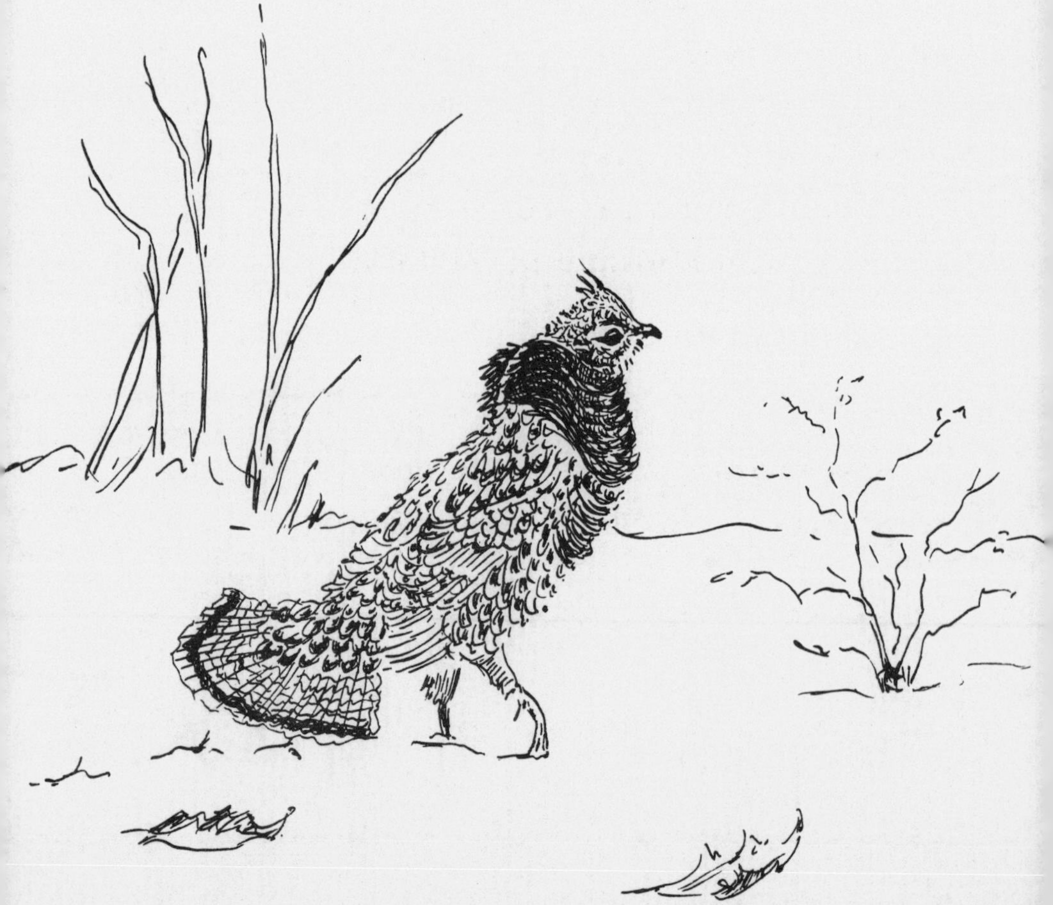

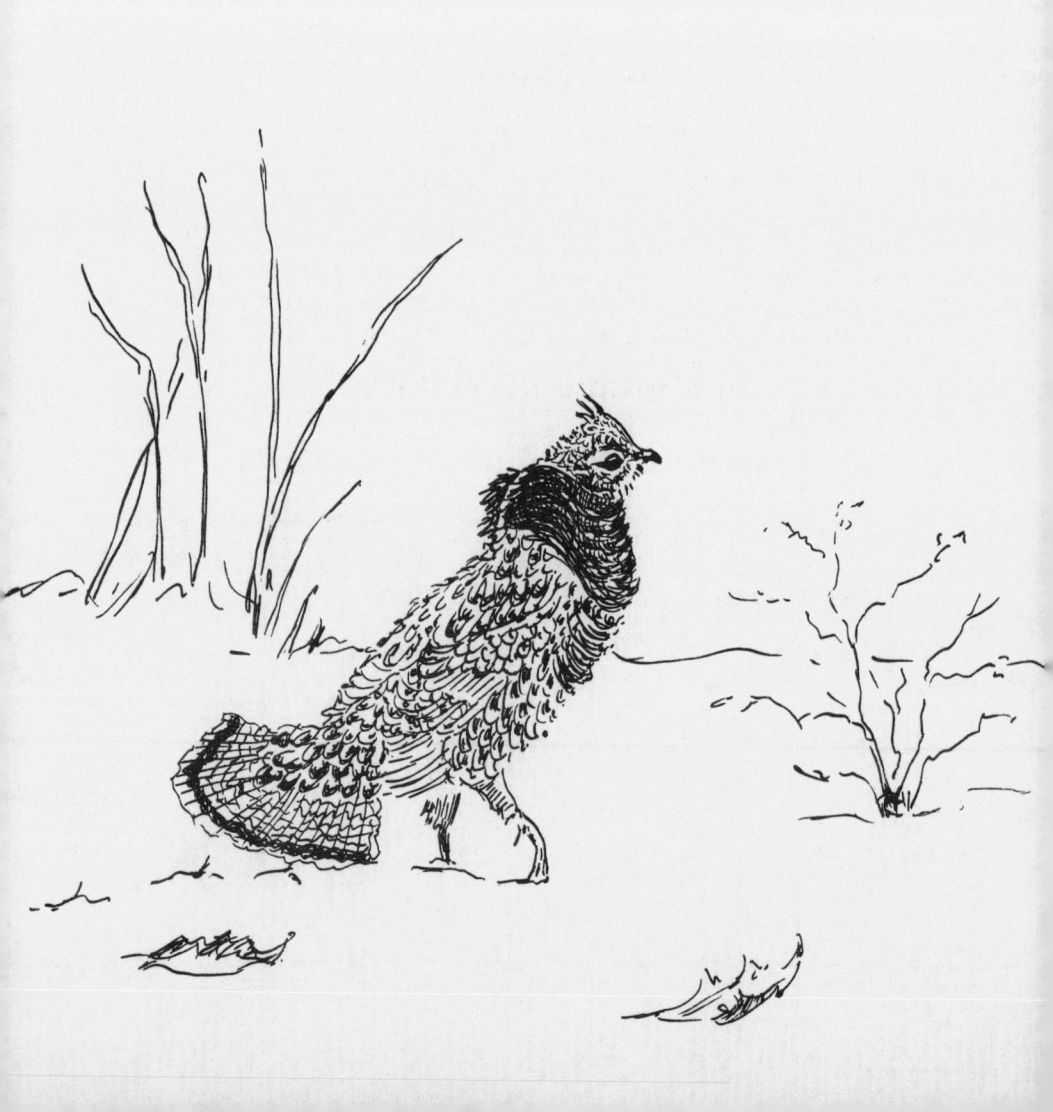

Ruffed Grouse

When my courting urge comes round,
I whir my wings and thump the ground.
People say it sounds like muffled thunder,
but it is my call of love.
I like the fan-feathers you gave me, Lord,
a greenish-black ruff, like a fan,
so different!
As you know, Lord,
I am a game bird.
I hide in the forest for protection,
and you helped me know how to scare away intruders.
Even though I look more like a farm hen
than a bird,
I am content.
Blessings on you, dear Lord.

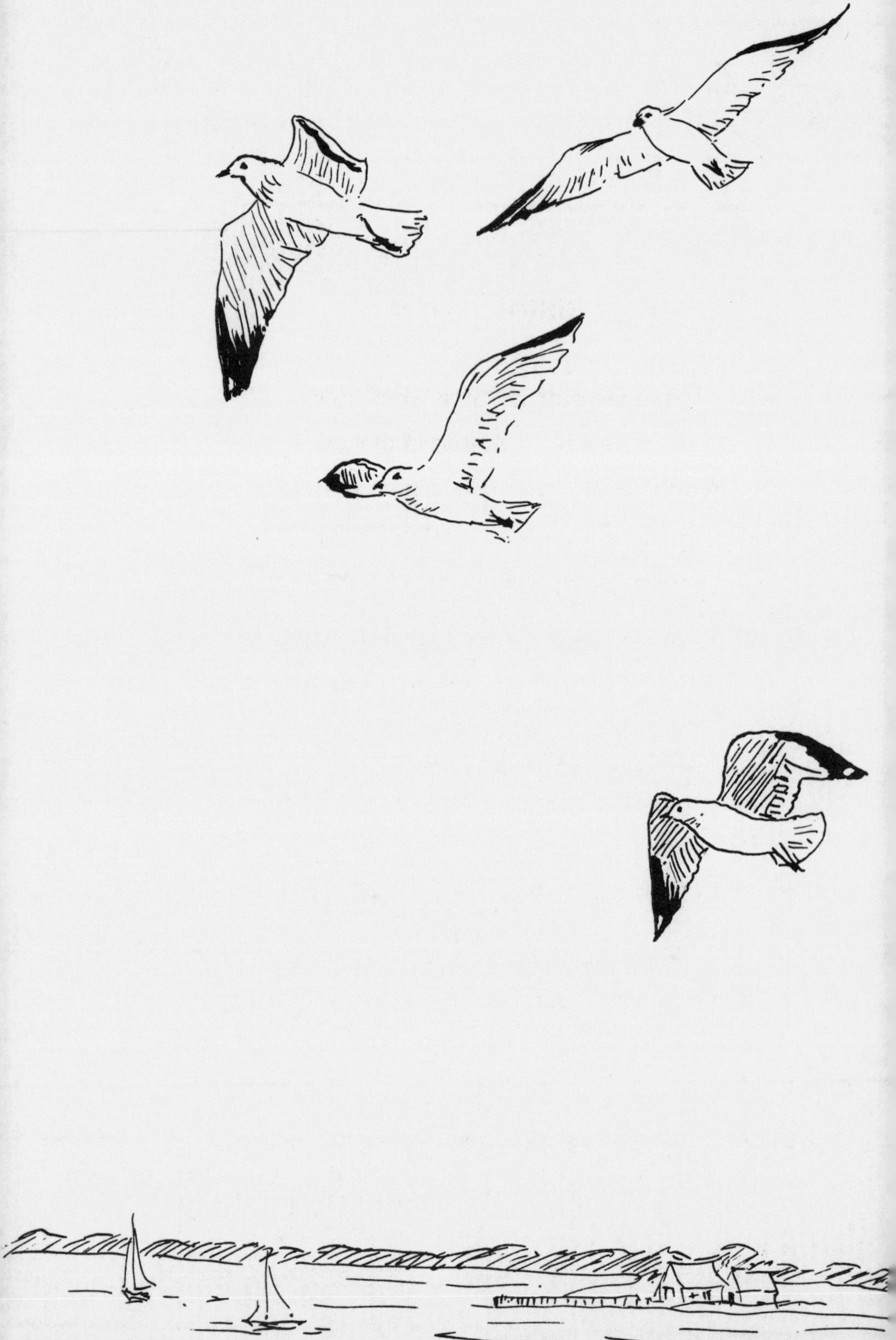

Seagull

Something has been bothering me, Lord.
It's that word "gullible."
Our family resents it.
We are not easily fooled.
We are intelligent and accomplished!
What other bird can weather the gales
of the fiercest hurricanes?
Our life is a joy,
dipping and soaring, dipping and soaring,
scarcely needing to move our wings.
And people on boats
toss us such delicious morsels.
But that word gullible is so bothersome, Lord.

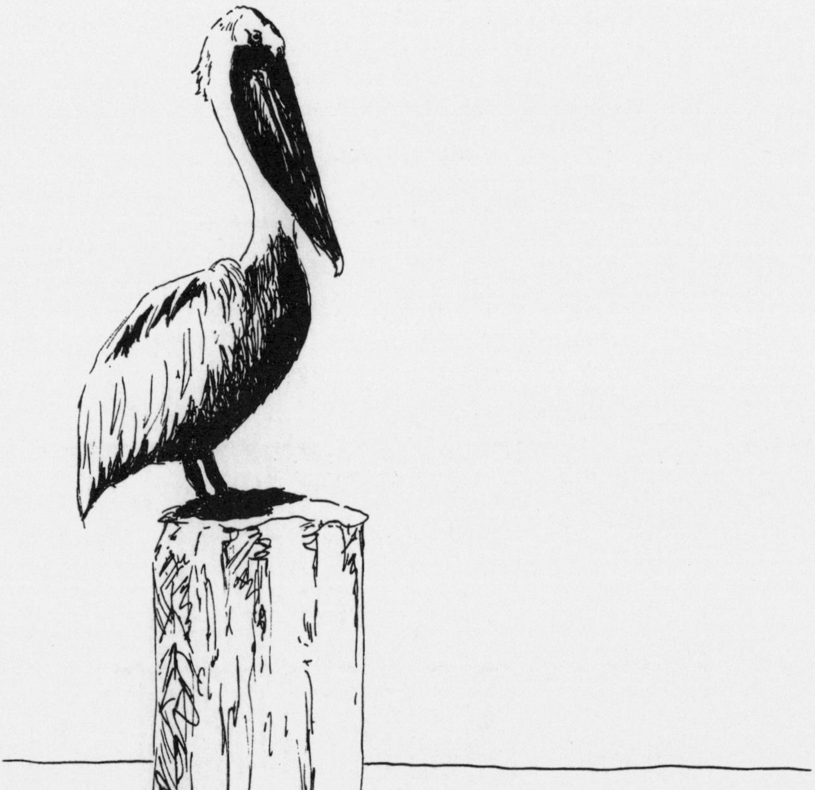

Pelican

The size of my big scooping bill
makes fishing a cinch.
It looks like the jai-a-lai basket
that catches those fast balls.
I simply go "flap-flap and scoop"
and I have my dinner!
I may be awkward on foot,
but I am a master at
flying and fishing skills.
I am so grateful that
you didn't make me a land bird, Lord.

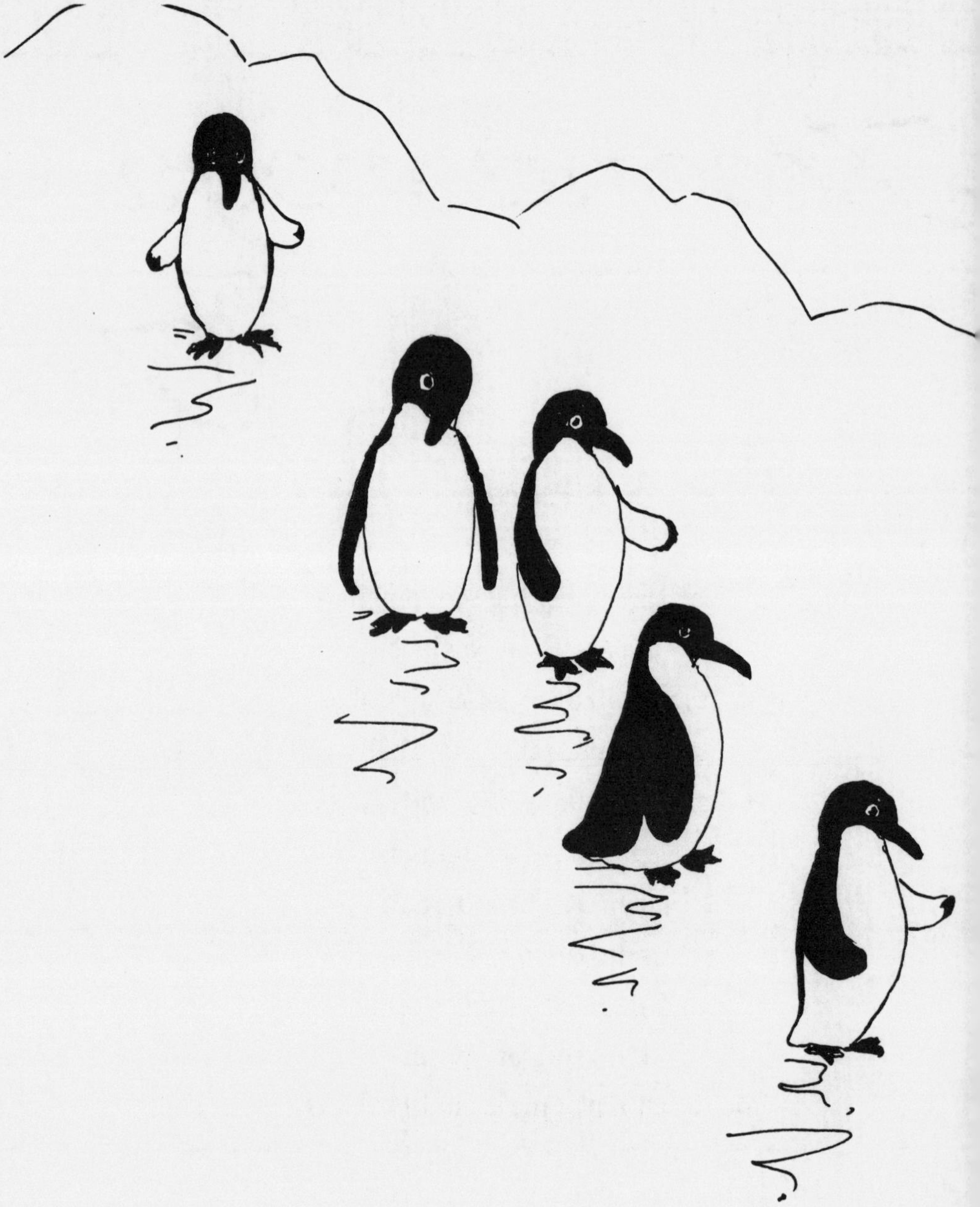

Penguin

I find, Lord, that some people
do not know what I am!
"A bird?" they ask,
"But he walks on rocks and ice,
and swims!"
Now <u>you</u> know what I am,
and <u>I</u> know what I am,
so it doesn't matter, does it?
Have you ever noticed, Lord,
how few people
know who they are?

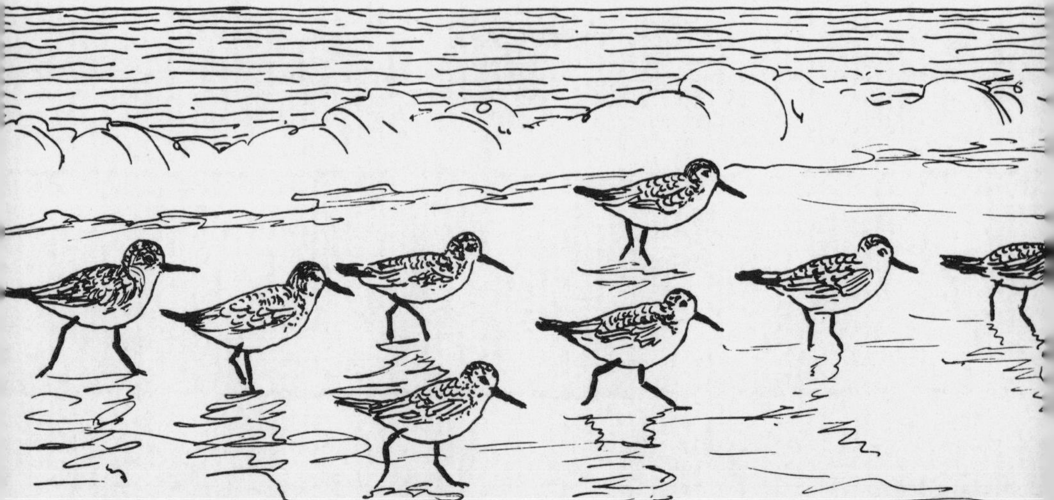

Sanderling

Thank you, God, for the sea
and all its washed-up, tasty-bits.
You were wise
to cover the earth
with so much water.
As I skirt the scalloped foam,
I often think that man, someday,
will get his food and power
from this same sea.
Don't they know that it should be
protected from pollution?
What a beautiful world you created for us!
Why do people mistreat it?

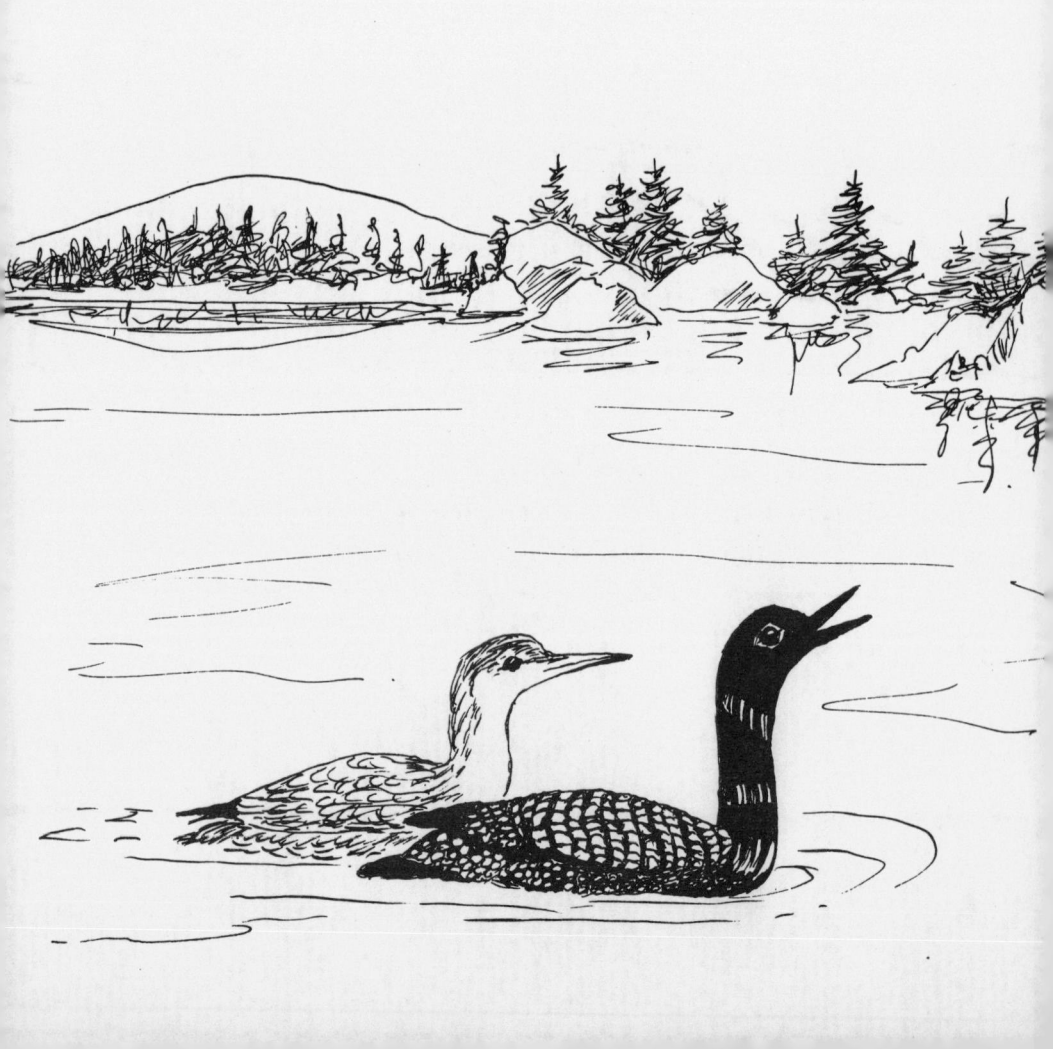

Loon

I've heard folks say
"crazy as a loon."
That's slander, Lord.
We are really quite brilliant.
We are water birds —
deep divers —
a hundred feet in submarine pursuit
is common.
Is that crazy?
Our eerie hoots may sound like
the laughter of demons
but not unlike the shrill voices
of some of those same people who say
"crazy as a loon!"

Swan

We are large water birds,
elegant and graceful.
Artists have painted us —
Ballerinas imitate
our grace and beauty.
You know we mate for life, Lord.
This year I am saddened.
My dear partner was killed
by thoughtless young people
in a speed boat.
That was right after
our five little signets were born.
I am devastated, Lord.

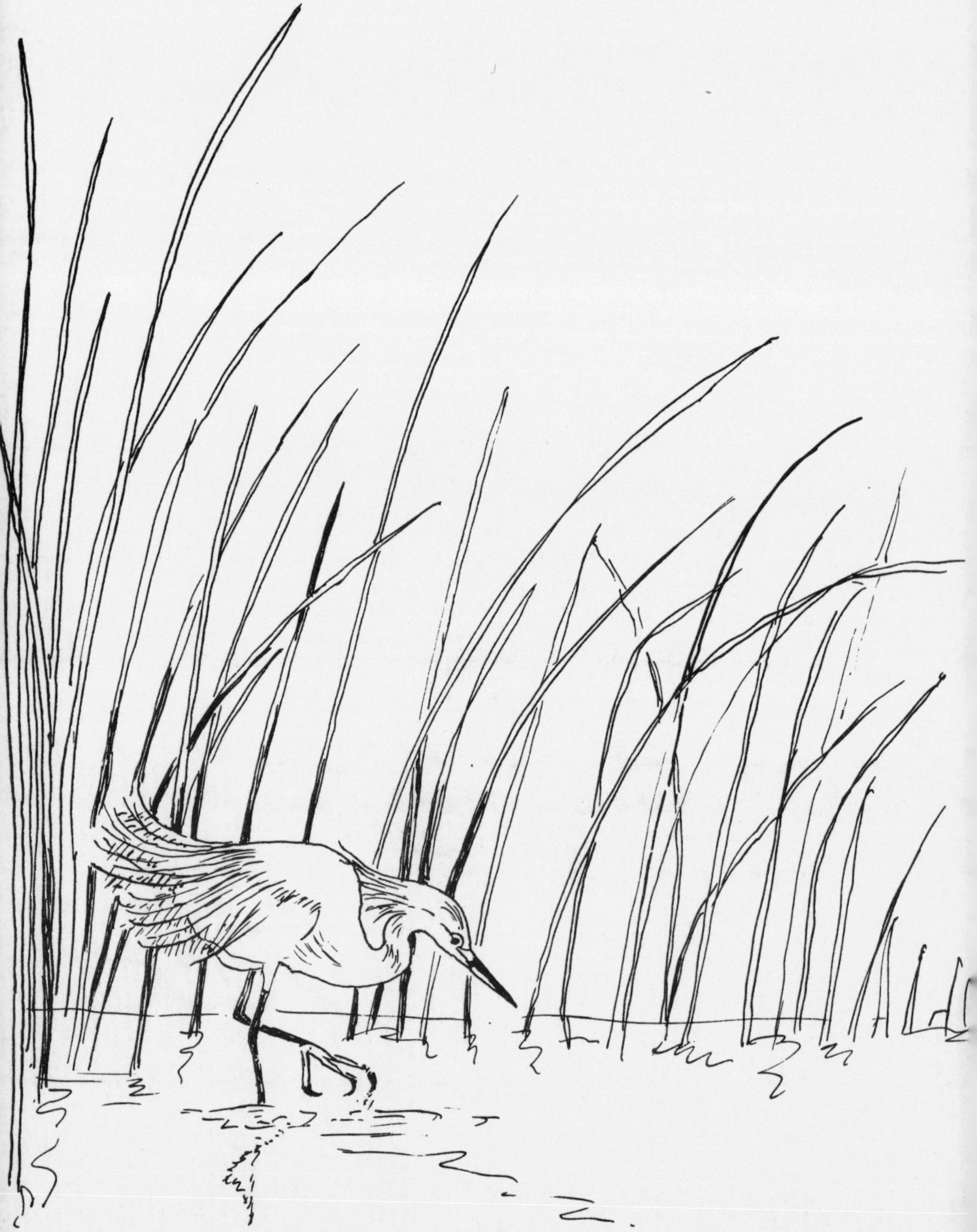

Snowy Egret

With our long, white, aigrette plumes,
slender black legs and yellow feet,
we are a striking sight
in the dull-colored marshes.
But not many of us are left.
Why, oh why, in years past
did plume-hunters kill us
for the millinery trade?
Artists enjoy painting us
as we stroll majestically
through the marshes
eating minnows, crawfish,
snakes and insects.
Please help people to understand
we need to keep
our marshes and our plumes.

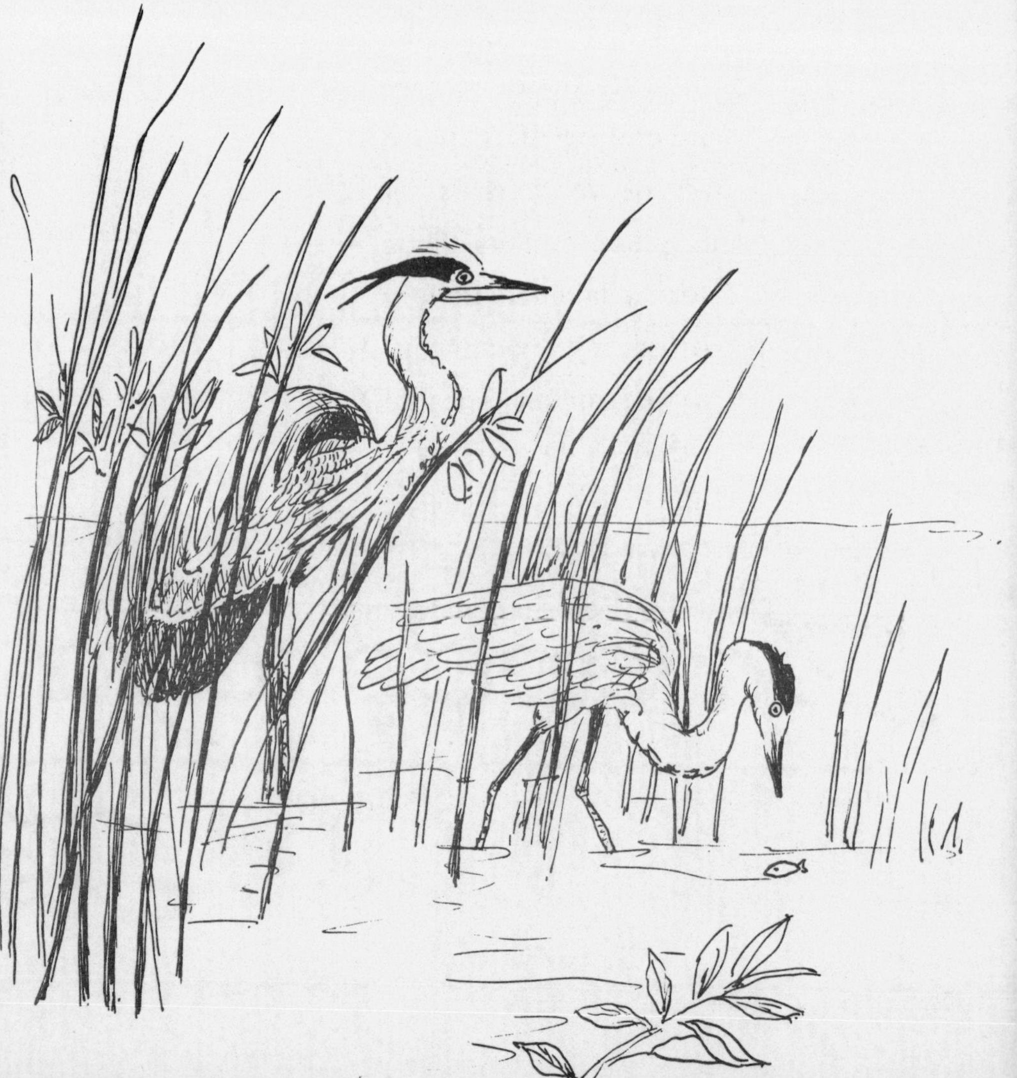

Great Blue Heron

I'm a proud American bird,
but I try to be humble.
Didn't you say "Blessed are the humble?"
I live on ponds and shallows,
inlets and estuaries,
salt-water and fresh water.
These waters are filled with excellent food—
tadpoles, frogs, salamanders,
snakes and fish.
Some call me a loner,
but I am happy in my solitude.
My stilt-like legs
tread the marshlands safely,
and my long neck acts as a periscope
over the swaying grass.
How grateful I am to you, Lord,
for my marsh world.
But we are rapidly losing our wetlands.
Why can't man realize what is happening?

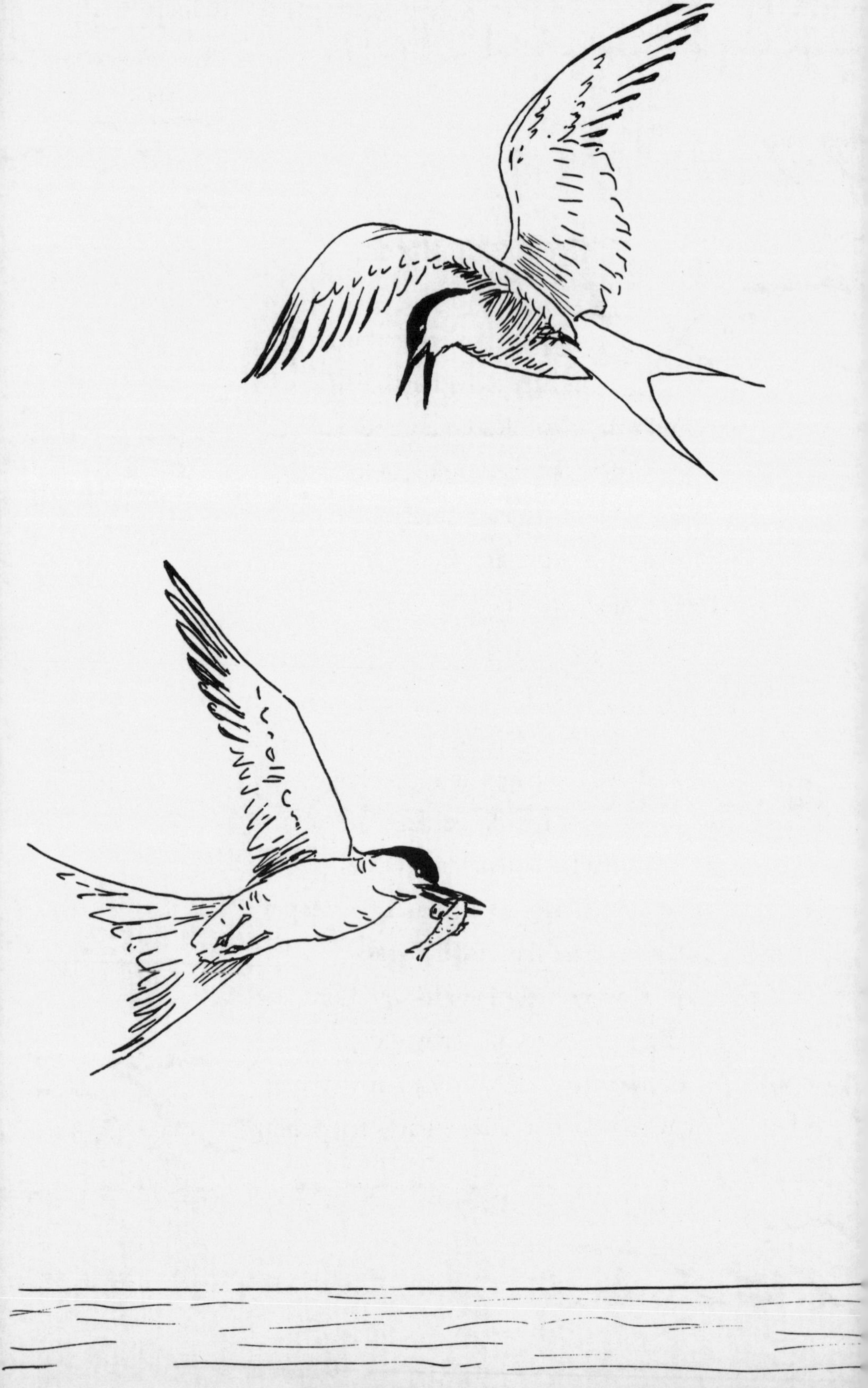

Common Tern

Many nature lovers say
that we are the most graceful
of all the shore birds,
with our forked tails,
and streamlined bodies.
We dine on minnows and insects.
Fishermen like us.
We help them locate schools of fish.
Though my home is nothing to brag about —
a depression in sand and shells
along a beach,
we have a devoted family life.
My mate and I share chores,
even incubation!
Our children stay with us
and we are loyal to our families.
This you have taught us, Lord,
"Kee-urr".

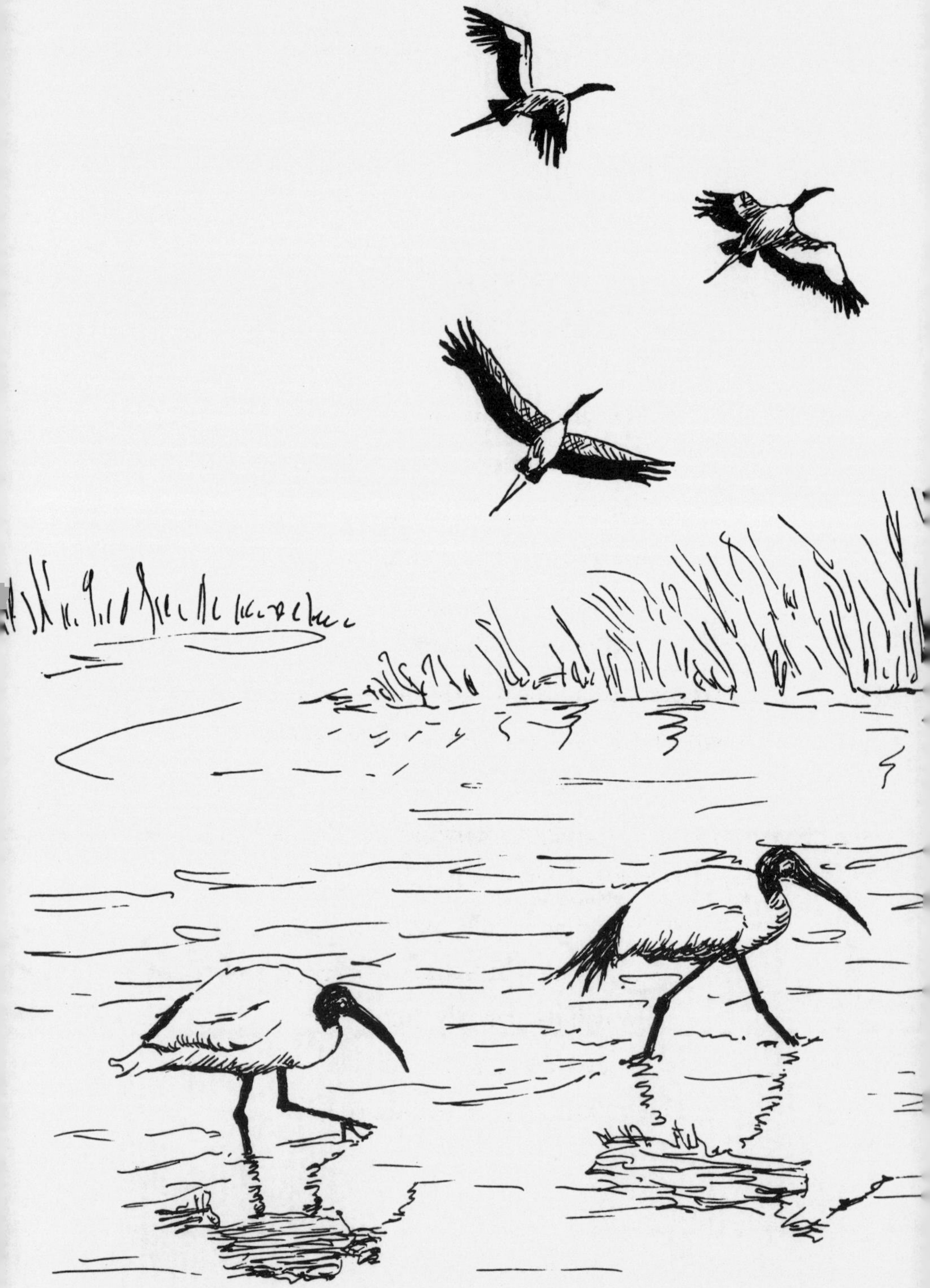

Woodstork

We are waders,
and one of America's largest birds.
Our chief nesting ground
has been the Florida Everglades.
There were thousands of us at one time.
Now only a few remain.
Water was the gift of the Everglades.
Today it is polluted and disappearing.
Please tell the developers
and the unthinking to save our wetlands.
Why do men cut our trees and drain our wetlands?
How can we convince people that
our nesting habitat must be preserved?
Can't people see that
if birds die,
human existence is threatened too?

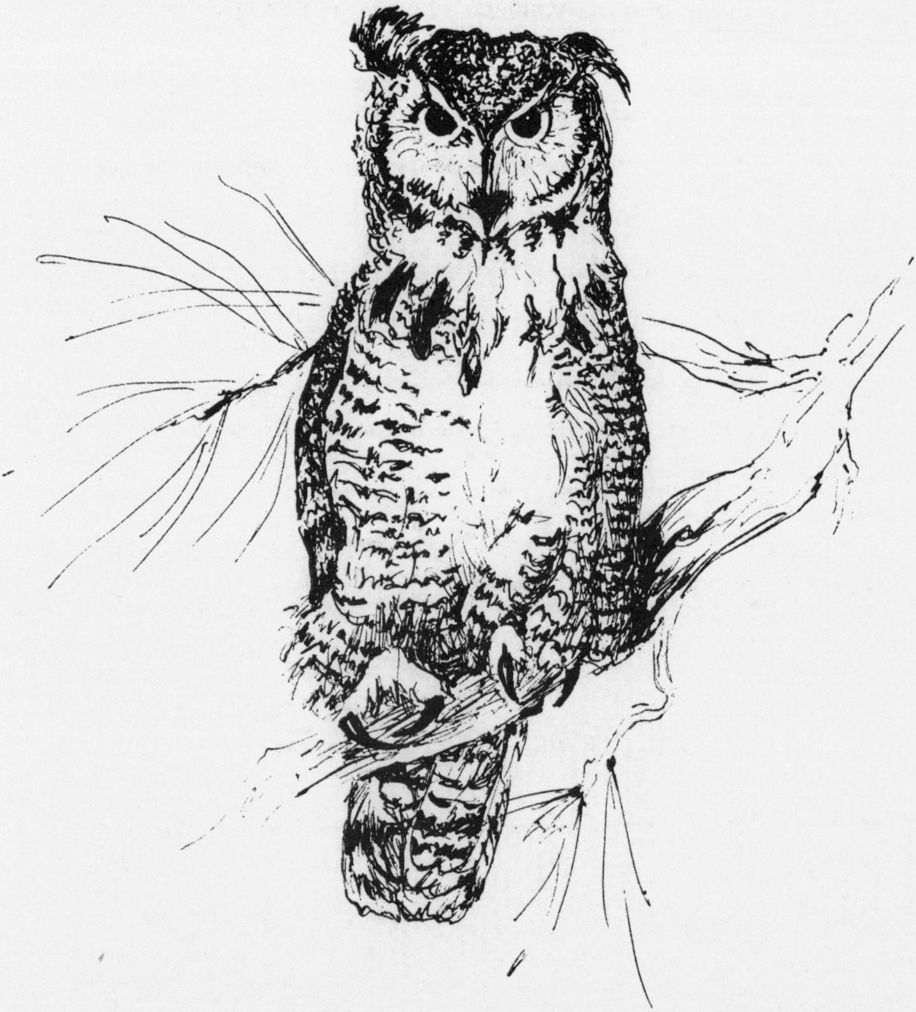

Epilogue
by
The Owl

And now, dear friends, since you have listened to some of our intimate conversations with God, do you not see what I meant in the preface when I said that birds and man have similar traits?

I believe that we are all meant to be here for a purpose: the Eagle, for instance, boastful as he is, teaches us to soar -- to carry out our dreams -- the Dove is the symbol of peace and love. And the little Chickadee expresses the joy of living by sharing his gladness. Yes, even that sour-faced Raven must have a reason for living.

I hate to say it, Lord, but man is our biggest problem for only he can control our wetlands, tree cutting, pollution and insecticides. He is ruining our natural resources, and let us remember that extinction is forever!

Please help us respect God's natural needs and beauties before it is too late.

For Your Own Bird Notes

For Your Own Bird Notes

For Your Own Bird Notes